D1518098

Linking Technology and Curriculum
Integrating the ISTE NETS Standards into Teaching and Learning

Second Edition

Jeri A. Carroll

Tonya L. Witherspoon
Witchita State University

Merrill
Prentice Hall

Upper Saddle River, New Jersey
Columbus, Ohio

Vice President and Publisher: Jeffery W. Johnston
Acquisitions Editor: Debra A. Stollenwerk
Production Editor: Kimberly J. Lundy
Design Coordinator: Diane C. Lorenzo
Cover Designer: Thomas Borah
Production Manager: Pamela D. Bennett
Director of Marketing: Ann Castel Davis
Marketing Manager: Krista Groshong
Marketing Services Manager: Barbara Koontz

Pearson Education Ltd., *London*
Pearson Education Australia Pty. Limited, *Sydney*
Pearson Education Singapore Pte. Ltd.
Pearson Education North Asia Ltd., *Hong Kong*
Pearson Education Canada, Ltd., *Toronto*
Pearson Educación de Mexico, S.A. de C.V.
Pearson Education— Japan, *Tokyo*
Pearson Education Malaysia Pte. Ltd.
Pearson Education, *Upper Saddle River, New Jersey*

Selected lessons adapted and reprinted with permission of the International Society for Technology in Education (ISTE), 800-336-5191 (US & Canada) or 541-302-3777 (Int'l), iste@iste.org, www.iste.org. All rights reserved. Permission does not constitute an endorsement by ISTE.

10 9 8 7 6 5 4
ISBN 0-13-097108-1

This book is dedicated to teachers and students striving to make decisions about what's best for learners, searching for ways to avoid becoming overwhelmed in an age where there is rapid development of emerging technologies.

But, especially, this book is dedicated to the curriculum and technology specialist teams that work together sharing the best of both worlds to make a real difference integrating technology into the curriculum.

As teachers, embrace your tech support person and allow them into your classroom as a true team member.

PREFACE

This book is designed for educators interested in integrating the National Educational Technology Standards for Students established by the International Society for Technology in Education (ISTE NETS*S) into their classroom activities. In doing so, the ISTE National Educational Standards for Teachers will also be accomplished. The text provides ideas for supporting teacher productivity and regular classroom instruction with technology as well as creative ways to use technology in classrooms with students.

We start with the authors' technology stories— how they got to where they are in using technology— and suggest that as you read the book you formulate your own story. In each story is something unique that may lead others in making decisions and trying new things.

Following the stories, readers are encouraged to (1) locate technology in their classrooms and schools, (2) learn to use what students will have to use, (3) learn to use technology tools to make their own lives simpler, (4) learn to use technology tools with students, and (5) learn the legal and ethical issues surrounding the use of technology in schools.

Ideas for using common technology tools in English/language arts, math, science, and social studies provide teachers with ways to weave technology into the content and technology standards with materials, equipment, and software usually found in the classroom. Integrated lessons also include standards in art, music, health and physical education. These lessons were collected from a variety of sources including the International Society for Technology in Education (ISTE), as in the first edition of this book, classroom teachers, colleagues, and several brainstorming sessions. The common tools include spreadsheets, word processors, the Internet, digital imaging, and hypermedia tools.

Finally, this text presents content and technology standards, online resources, standards organizations and Web sites, and other resources to help teachers link technology to instruction in meaningful ways.

ACKNOWLEDGMENTS
Thanks to the following people for their assistance with this book:
- **Debbie Stollenwerk**, for her invitation, assistance, and patience.
- **Rick Weaver, Steve Witherspoon**, and **Karen Reynolds** for their content and editorial comments.
- Colleagues at Wichita State University, ISTE, USD 259, and ESSDACK who have encouraged us in the creation of activities for this book.
- **Tom Carroll,** the US Department of Education, and the United States Government for the PT3 initiative, which took us to the water, and when we wouldn't drink, pushed us in.
- Our families for their prodding, patience, and love.

ABOUT THE AUTHORS

Jeri Carroll is Professor of Elementary and Early Childhood Education at Wichita State Universit,y where she has been teaching for 19 years. Jeri has degrees in music education, elementary education, and early childhood education and 15 years of public school teaching experience and is presently the curriculum resource specialist on WSU's PT3 grant, Models, Mentors, and Mobility: Project M3. She enjoys her family (stepson, wife, and grandson and her two girls), friends, and traveling.

While in the first year of the grant, Jeri met Tonya Witherspoon when she needed help setting up a Web site for the grant's first major project, Technology Integration Projects for Students (TIPS). What Jeri didn't realize was how much more she needed Tonya than as a Web master. It wasn't long before Tonya and Jeri began working as a team on many projects they undertook: Jeri's education classes where Tonya helped with technology, or Tonya's technology classes where Jeri helped with curriculum, each seeking and valuing the other's input.

Tonya Witherspoon is the Web master for WSU's Project M3. She has worked with technology for the past 15 years, the past 10 of them in various schools as a volunteer and consultant. She has expertise in technology hardware and software, programming, and design. Her family has representatives in all school levels: preschool (one daughter) elementary school (two boys), middle schools (two boys), high school (her husband Steve is chair of the social studies department for the IB program at East High School in Wichita), and the university where Tonya is completing her general studies degree with an emphasis in computing technology and telecommunications.

This book is an example of a curriculum specialist and a technology specialist collaborating as a team, working, learning, and creating together.

CONTENTS

TECHNOLOGY INTEGRATION: SETTING THE STAGE

Where Are You on Your Technology Journey?

Everyone has a technology story. The stories tell about your own levels of adoption (see p. 9 for an explanation of the levels of adoption) and the journey through them. You might not think you use technology because if it has been a true tool in your work, the memory of the technology might fade to the background of the project, as it should. If you begin to recall the machines and tools you've used, you will probably surprise yourself. We all have a problem staying up with new technologies and sometimes want to throw in the towel and say it is an impossible job. But again, as you think over your technology story, many of the tools you have used are probably already outdated. You have probably already adapted to many new generations of tools yourself. Learning about new technologies and how to use them is possible.

It is important that you think about where you are on your own technology journey, so we have decided to share our stories with you. After you read them, think about or write your own and you will see that your background is not void of technology. When you see you have moved through a generation or two of machines, you will have more confidence in adding new technology to your repertoire. See if you can identify different levels of adoption in our stories.

Jeri Carroll

Typewriters. My mom was a legal secretary and my dad a music teacher. I took typing classes my mom made me take, the first one in junior high and a complete secretarial training course in high school. I worked in offices during the summers and learned to run ditto and mimeograph machines, and to splice and repair the films that were shown in the schools. I used a manual typewriter during my undergraduate work and an electric typewriter for graduate school.

Fortran. Nine years of teaching took me back to college (1973) for my doctorate. No foreign language for me. I took Fortran and keypunched many cards for the mainframe computer to complete my dissertation data analysis.

Microcomputers. During the summer of 1983, I took a parent/student computer class with my sixth-grade stepson, Matt. We worked on Apple IIes and I was hooked. Within a week or so, we had one at home with a Muppet Learning Keys Pad for 2-year-old Callie (I still have the Muppet Pad, not the IIe). Later in the 80s, the Macintoshes hit the market and they really made sense to me. I bought one for my office and left the Apple IIe at home for Matt, Callie, and Molly. I've been through several generations of Macs at work and home. And a couple of PCs, too.

Integrating Technology. I eventually got e-mail and started sending everyone e-mail— even to the people who have an office next door to me. And then there was the Internet— that story is later in the Internet section of this book. Two years ago, I worked with a group at WSU to write a grant on integrating technology into teacher education which we received, and I have been hooked ever since. The new standards for our accreditation agency (NCATE) included a stronger emphasis on technology. I was teaching an Introduction to Education course at the time the challenge arrived. I decided that I could not only use technology in the college classroom, but actually set up situations where during class they walked down the hall to the computer lab as part of four learning centers set up in the classroom. That was easy, but then along came "The Cart!"

The Multimedia Cart. Our Educational Computing Coordinator and the head of our Technology Staff came to a faculty meeting to demonstrate "The Cart," I went away from the demonstration overwhelmed. All I could recall was that the "on" button was clearly marked and I should let the projector fan continue to run to cool the projector. The cart could do a lot of things— most of which I couldn't. I was committed to seeing that our students became technologically proficient. When I asked the two technology gurus to do a demonstration of the cart for one of my teacher education courses, they suggested it would be better if I used it to teach my students something. After putting up a bit of an argument, I decided I could do it. I worked through PowerPoint— alone in my office where no one could see— and I learned to insert a CD into my computer. Finally, I figured out how to switch from the computer to the CD player, to the video on the cart, and back to the computer. I was ready.

The Demonstration— Fearless Faculty. The day came. I was there early. Everything was set. I felt quite comfortable. I could use that cart! As I walked to my office, I suddenly realized I didn't have a back-up plan if the cart crashed. I got hives all around my neck. Not to deter me. I was ready. I pulled up the PowerPoint presentation, switched to the video segment, back to the PowerPoint, a switch to the CD-ROM, and back to PowerPoint for the conclusion. A final switch to Word to show the formatted paper. I did it!

The Result— Fearless Students. The most important part of this entire episode was the result. Three weeks later, students were scheduled to do presentations. The first two groups asked to have the cart scheduled. I was impressed. I scheduled it for the other two groups just in case. All four groups of students used the cart! It worked. Modeling something with ease showed students its value and empowered them to move ahead.

Wireless. We've now gone wireless in our building. We roll mobile labs into any classroom. We're hoping to hook our PDAs to the wireless network. I've ventured into using Macs and PCs. I work in FrontPage. I've digitized video. I bought a digital camera. I'm eyeing that Robotics course Tonya teaches. We're writing a book to help others learn to use technology. And, my own children haven't caught up with me yet. I'm just waiting for whatever comes next. Whatever it brings, I'm ready!

Tonya Witherspoon

My first experience with technology was in the 1970s in my fourth grade typing class. When class began, our teacher told us to look for the home row that began with a, s, d, f. I looked down and my keyboard was blank. I raised my hand and told my teacher that my typewriter was broken; it had no letters on the keys. She clapped and exclaimed brightly that I was going to be the best typist in the class because I was the lucky one who sat at the only typewriter that didn't have labeled keys. I was surprised and a little wary but up to the challenge: I found a page in our typing book that labeled the keys for me, found home row, and began typing. I quickly became one of the most proficient typists in our class. *Typing allowed me to quickly make my reports neater and more professional looking.*

I didn't actually use a computer until the 1980s in high school when I took a pilot class, "Computer Algebra." After each new theorem we learned in class, we programmed the computer to follow the same steps and solve the problem in BASIC. Writing these programs was like writing a series of instructions in what I thought of as a secret code. Writing this code for the computer helped me understand the logic and steps in solving algebraic problems.

When I was in college, I worked for a small business keeping the books using an IBM computer (before Windows). We used DOS, and much to my surprise, the BASIC code I had learned in high school worked on this machine as well. I wrote several programs to help me keep track of expenses, income, and other necessary business accounts. I worked for a couple of years and used the computer to type all correspondence, generate invoices, write checks, and maintain all the business records. I liked the efficiency and speed of this tool, and *it greatly helped me do my job.*

My next job was Children's Education Director at a church and I dealt mostly with crayons, glue, and construction paper. When our secretary quit abruptly, the pastor told the staff that our paychecks might be late because no one knew how to run the office computer. I volunteered to give it a try. It seemed that our paychecks were being held hostage by a machine that no one knew how to run. I booted it up, looked through the program menu, read the help file and by that afternoon I was printing payroll checks. There was a reason to use this technology— everyone needed a check and *I couldn't lose anything by trying.*

After using the computer in the office, I began to use it for my work, too. I created a database of all of my students and families. I mail-merged this to create mailing labels. I created a database for curriculum and supplies. I used the computer to make fliers, posters, and handouts. I had done all of this work before with magic markers, clip art, and a copy machine. *I could now do this work faster and it looked better.* My appreciation of computers multiplied!

After working several years at the church I took a job as a systems administrator for the same small company I'd worked at during college. The business had grown and had many computers networked together. I was in charge of keeping them running, installing the hardware and software, and training the employees.

I donated time weekly at my children's school to keeping their computers running. The turning point came when Mrs. Bunk, my son's kindergarten teacher, asked for help. The PTA had purchased the kindergarten class a computer that included a software package. Mrs. Bunk thought the software wasn't appropriate for kindergartners because it required too much reading and wondered what I thought. I'd researched and chosen business software packages many times, but I had never really thought about educational software. However, after teaching at church for so many years and having five children myself, I was very intrigued with what children could do with a computer.

I spent an afternoon in WSU's computer lab and was amazed! They had a variety of educational software available. The first thing I looked at were Living Books, books that come alive in front of your very eyes! I knew that they were something the kindergartners would enjoy and would learn from. I purchased several and took them to school. They were a success!

I had done much work with businesses trying to find the best tools to help them with their jobs, but helping educators was the most rewarding thing I had ever done. Instead of being more productive and seeing the bottom line get fatter, I was actually helping to shape children and see their minds grow. I soon began consulting and helping other schools, starting websites, helping teachers use grade book packages, PowerPoint, robotics, and clay animation— the list is long and expanding. *I saw children come alive and learn in a way that was exciting.*

I am currently working at Wichita State University for a PT3 grant— Preparing Tomorrow's Teachers to Use Technology. We are using wireless mobile laptop labs, handheld computers, digital imaging, robotics, the Internet and much more. I wanted to go back to Mrs. Bunk's room and see if this new technology was going to make a big difference in the kindergarten classroom where I'd found my first success. I took a set of wireless laptops and set up a computer center in the classroom during center time. When Mrs. Bunk introduced me she said, "Class, Mrs. Witherspoon is here with some very special computers. They don't have any wires and they are small and we can carry them anywhere we want to work." One boy raised his hand and said, "Mrs. Bunk, those are called laptops." It was obvious that the students were natives when it came to computers. The computer center was a hit. The children were very comfortable at their table and chairs, it was easy for them to rotate from center to center, and the activity was engaging. However, the computer center in Mrs. Bunk's classroom was just one more way to learn among the clay, crayons, markers, and books. This is how it should be, *incorporating new, effective tools into the process of learning.*

Technology and the Curriculum: Integrating ISTE Standards

Technology has been here for a long time, it's here to stay, and there's more on the way. The tools commonly and not-so-commonly found in schools provide valuable methods for researching topics (CD-ROMs, online encyclopedias, world-wide Internet resources), analyzing information (spreadsheets, databases, graphs, timelines, calculators), and communicating (word processing, online dictionaries, digital imaging, e-mail, discussion boards, listservs).

Technology teaches us a valuable lesson. It sits there waiting patiently to hook us. It allows us to attack a problem and solve it. We only need to watch a young child with a new piece of technology, try it, investigate it, explore it, and use it to know how we should do it ourselves. The parents, community, school boards, and legislators have provided some resources to get us started. However, some of the more stubborn ones will quickly say, "You can lead a horse to water, but you can't make it drink." The nation's leading curriculum and technology organizations have now all integrated technology into their standards or principles. Accreditation of P–16 schools rests on addressing the standards of the organizations. So, even as the horse can't be made to drink, it can be pushed into the water. We have taken the plunge! Technology teaches us to not be afraid of new things, to not be stubborn, and that you can teach an old dog new tricks!

The National Technology Plan

The US Department of Education outlines its technology goals in *e-Learning: Putting a World-class Education at the Fingertip of All Children: A National Education Technology Plan* (2001) (http://www.ed.gov/Technology/elearning/e-learning.pdf).

Goal 1: All students and teachers will have access to information technology in their classrooms, schools, communities and homes.

Goal 2: All teachers will use technology effectively to help students achieve high academic standards.

Goal 3: All students will have technology and information literacy skills.

Goal 4: Research and evaluation will improve the next generation of technology applications for teaching and learning.

Goal 5: Digital content and networked applications will transform teaching and learning.

National Technology Standards

The national organizations for English/language arts (NCTE and IRA), math (NCTM), science (NAS NRC), and social studies (NCSS) all include technology as a component of their standards. In addition, the International Society for Technology in Education (ISTE) recently developed National Educational Technology Standards for Students (NETS*S) and National Educational Technology Standards for Teachers (NETS*T). ISTE has also worked with a collaborative to develop Technology Standards for School Administrators (TSSA). The collaborative included the National School Boards Association National Association of Elementary School Principals; National Association of Secondary

School Principals; ISTE; the Consortium for School Networking; the North Central Regional Technology Consortium/North Central Regional Educational Laboratory; the Southern Regional Education Board; the Kentucky Department of Education; the Mississippi Department of Education; the Principals' Executive Program–University of North Carolina; and the College of Education–Western Michigan University.

ISTE NETS for Students
The ISTE NETS*S cover six broad topics: (1) basic operations and concepts, (2) social, ethical, and human issues, (3) technology productivity tools, (4) technology communications tools, (5) technology research tools, and (6) technology problem-solving and decision-making tools. Each of these standards has several indicators to more clearly outline expectations. ISTE has developed a collection of activities, *Connecting Curriculum and Technology*, for students that address content and technology standards, affectionately called the "Chubby" book. (See the ISTE Web site for more information: http://www.iste.org).

ISTE NETS for Teachers
The ISTE NETS*T cover four profiles (general education, preservice education, student teaching, and first year teaching) in six broad topics: (1) technology operations and concepts, (2) planning and designing learning environments and experiences, (3) teaching, learning, and the curriculum, (4) assessment and evaluation, (5) productivity and professional practice, and (6) social, ethical, legal and human issues. Indicators provide guidance for implementation of the standards. A companion book, *Preparing Teachers to Use Technology* (2001), provides guidelines and activities for colleges of education to use with preservice teacher education students as they explore and learn to teach with and about technology.

Technology Standards for School Administrators
TSSA provides a framework for school administrators. At the time of comment during the 2001 National Educational Computing Conference (NECC) sponsored by the National Educational Computing Association (NECA), TSSA contained six standards: (1) leadership, (2) learning and teaching, (3) productivity and professional practice, (4) support, management, and operations, (5) assessment and evaluation, and (6) social, legal, and ethical issues. Discussion focused on the need for collaboration and advocacy in developing a vision, mission, and implementation plans for technology use in schools.

This text provides one avenue for students, teachers, and administrators to link technology and curriculum, addressing curriculum and technology standards through meaningful, content-based, classroom activities.

LOCATING AND TESTING TECHNOLOGY IN SCHOOLS

Wherever you are observing, tutoring, student teaching, or teaching, the first step you must take to be able to use technology in the classroom is to note what is available, determine what technology and skills the students have, locate the curriculum standards and supporting materials (including content specific hardware and software), attempt to connect everything, and learn to use it. As part of the **ISTE NETS*T (Standard 1)**, you will be required to "demonstrate a sound understanding of technology operations and concepts."

Asking Questions During the Job Interview

During a job interview, or when you take a position in the school, ask the interview team or principal a simple, open-ended question about technology: "How is technology used in your school?" This leaves it wide open for them to tell you what they have. Follow-up questions to their response might include

- What kind of tech support is available?
- Is there a secure computer for teacher use?
- Are the student computers networked?
- Do all student computers have access to the Internet?
- What policies exist for the use of technology with students?
- What type of firewall or filter has been installed to monitor students' Internet access to safe sites?
- How often are equipment and software updated?
- What are the policies for replacement of equipment?
- What software is available in the building?
- Where else might software be borrowed for classroom use?
- How are requests for equipment and software made?
- What types of technology tools are required for teachers to use, i.e. grading software, communication, reporting, etc.?
- Which teachers serve as mentors for other teachers?
- Are there "Gen www.Y" student mentors available for teachers?

Taking a Technology Inventory in the Schools

Once you are in the school, take a walk through it to see what technology is readily visible. Find a veteran teacher to talk with and tell them what you have seen and ask if there are other things in the school that you should be aware of. In addition, ask if there are ways to secure temporary use of other equipment, i.e., checking out an overhead projector for a day, securing listening labs from a district source, borrowing microscopes from a science center. Ask to see a copy of the school's Acceptable Use Policy (AUP) and technology plan.

Taking a Classroom Technology Inventory

Look around for what is readily seen in the classroom and for what may be stored in closets or cupboards. Make sure that everything is in good working condition and if it is not, take it to the office and file a written request to have it fixed. Learn to use it, if you don't already know how.

Setting Up and Testing Hardware

Learn to set up and use all the equipment in the classroom. Start with the simple and move to the more complex. Do not assume that because you have a VCR at home, you will be able to operate the VCR in the classroom. Each one is different. Try everything out during the days before the students come. If something doesn't work, take it to the office and fill out a written request to have it repaired (usually called a work order). Periodically check on the status.

If there is a computer in the classroom or a computer station, examine all the connections. Follow the wires from the main unit to all the peripherals. If there is a chance you will have to dismantle and reconnect the various pieces, make it easy for yourself. The cables usually have appropriate markings on them to help guide assembly. However, if they are difficult to see, consider marking cables and slots with matching colored tape.

Setting Up and Testing Software

Examine any software available in the classroom or for checkout in a central location. Make note of what titles you are familiar with and how they might be used in your classroom. Check with other teachers to see what they have and what their favorites are. Make an effort to try out a few titles that are new to you and see how they might support your curriculum. Set up a spreadsheet to help log and sort the software titles. Procedures for evaluating software are located elsewhere in this book.

Evaluating Software

When evaluating software you must consider functionality, usability, and purpose. First of all, check the system requirements and make sure that the software can be loaded and will run on the equipment that you have. Does it have a good help file, a tutorial? Does it meet the needs of your curriculum and enhance your instruction? A more detailed list of things to consider is located elsewhere in this book.

Assessing the Skills and Needs of Students

When your students arrive, find out what they can and cannot do. A listing of all the technology equipment in the room and a check-off sheet would help you in gaining this information. Reviewing skills that students should already have mastered by using some of the technology in your classroom is a good way to determine students' technology level. By using content that is familiar you can more easily determine technology skills.

USING TECHNOLOGY IN THE CLASSROOM

Most adults are well on their journey to using technology in teaching without even realizing it. We use it and experience it everyday— the telephone and cell phone, television and VCRs with cable and satellite connections, word processing equipment, and more recently, computers, e-mail, and the Internet. We're moving toward smart cars, smart homes, and can dream of what a smart school might be like. However, most of us are being asked to help students become literate in the use of technology and in gathering and reporting information in ways that we never experienced as students ourselves. As teachers, we are being asked to be travel guides on a journey we have never taken. But, we can do it!

Novice and Expert Learners

In his recent speeches, Tom Carroll, US Department of Education, Director of Preparing Tomorrow's Teachers to Use Technology (PT³), capitalizes on the concept of lifelong learning. He says that in today's schools we are all learners. As students and teachers, some of us are novice learners and some are expert learners. And those roles change periodically throughout the day. At times, teachers are put in the uncomfortable position of being a novice learner in their own classrooms, especially in the area of technology where students may be far more proficient than the teachers. If we can accept the role of novice learner in a classroom and allow students that expert role, we can use the knowledge and skills others on our "tour" have, even when we are the assigned guide.

Levels of Adoption

We will approach this section of the book like a typical teacher's journey into the unknown, recognizing that anxiety and fear may be two important factors to overcome. We start with the simplest of tools and go to the complex, tying this journey to research on the teachers' five levels of adoption for technology use: entry, adoption, adaptation, appropriation, and invention. http://www.apple.com/education/professionaldevelopment/tchrcenterstaff.html

The first level (entry) is one of getting started. It includes anxiety about technology use, even with those tools used most often: word processing, e-mail, and the Internet. The second level (adoption) involves increased teacher use of productivity tools and expanded use of word processing and e-mail, not yet requiring technology of students. The third level (adaptation) sees a faculty member using more technology in teaching and to teach. Video clips of instructional sequences might be posted online, Web-enhanced coursework is provided, and students will be required to use technology to complete required assignments. The fourth level (appropriation) allows for online collaboration in learning communities and a multifaceted approach to using technology. Level five (innovation) is reached when teachers begin to redesign their classrooms where technology is an integral part of all appropriate experiences, share their experience with others, and begin to advocate for systemic change.

Technology Tools and the ISTE Standards

What exactly do we mean by technology tools, especially in the educational setting? First, we know that tools are things that help us with our work. In education, then, technology tools are those machines and software that we use to accomplish tasks related to education. Roblyer and Ewards (2000) note that ". . . useful definitions of educational technology must focus on the process of applying tools for education purposes as well as the tools and materials used" (p. 6). Further, educational technology, is a "combination of the processes and tools involved in addressing education needs and problems, with an emphasis on applying the most current tools: computers and their related technologies."

As teachers, not only will you have to be able to use technology tools yourselves, but you will also need to require and/or train others to use them. These expectations are clearly outlined in the ISTE NETS for Teachers and Students.

As you learn to use technology for personal and professional use, you will meet the **ISTE NETS for Teachers** (ISTE NETS*T). As you provide experiences for students, you will help them meet the **ISTE NETS for Students** (ISTE NETS*S).

Developing a Technology Management Plan

ISTE NETS*T Standard 2 asks you to show competence to "plan and design effective learning environments and experiences supported by technology."

As part of your classroom management plan, include a section on technology management. Include how you would like students to care for and use the equipment and software in your classroom and in the building. Some things to think about:

- Have students wash their hands before touching the keyboard or other equipment. If there is not a sink in the classroom, keep moistened wipes or hand sanitizer nearby.
- Will students start and shut down computers?
- Will students work independently or in small groups?
- Will there be a limit on how long a student can use a computer at one sitting? If so, students can be trained to set and respond to a timer.
- If students work in pairs or small groups, how will their time be shared?
- Computers, along with all equipment in your room, need to be on a regular cleaning routine. Covering computers when not in use helps to keep them dust free, but it is still necessary to clean the screens, mice, and keyboards.
- At what times will students have access to computers? This will depend on the technology goals of the school and the configurations of computers available in the classroom and school.

Examining the School Computer Configurations

Computer use in the classroom usually falls into five categories: one computer, a small group of computers, a computer for everyone, a computer lab for class use, and wireless mobile labs.

Working in the One-Computer Classroom

If there is one computer in the classroom, it is usually for the teacher's use. The way it can be used for and with students will be linked to whether or not it is networked and if so, how it is linked to confidential information to which students should not have access. However, there are still ways it can be used with students.

Using One Computer as a Teaching Tool
Use the one computer in the classroom as a teaching tool:
- Keep records, manipulate information, produce individual letters to parents.
- Produce a class newsletter.
- Create customized follow-up work for lessons.
- Make personalized certificates of achievement.
- Create customized graphic organizers and instruction sheets.
- Create charts, student lists, and name tags.
- Communicate with other professionals and subject experts via e-mail.

Using One Computer as a Multimedia Chalkboard
Consider requesting a PC/Mac-to-TV scan converter to allow you to display what is on your computer screen on a TV. Another way to share one computer with many is to use an electronic whiteboard or a projector to project your computer screen on a wall or projection screen. With these additions you could:
- Demonstrate a process or procedure.
- Show pictures or a digitized video.
- Observe animals using Internet sites with Web cams.
- Write a class letter.
- Project images onto the whiteboard.
- "Show" a talking book.
- Share one software title with the entire class.
- Share an Internet site.
- Use as a learning center for center rotations in an integrated unit of study.

Working in the Five-Computer Classroom

Many elementary schools have attempted to have at least five computers in each classroom, networked and wired to the Internet. In middle schools and high schools, this usually first occurs in the language arts classrooms. Others that follow might include ESOL, foreign language, science, social studies, and maybe math. This five-computer configuration lends itself well to the use of learning stations in the classroom where one of the stations is the computer station. To use it as part of a learning station consider these possibilities:

Design a unit around a certain topic. Provide class activities to support learning about the topic. Rotate students through the stations as you would if there were no computer station. Initially, students may need more support and supervision, but as time goes by, they will become more independent and begin to help one another with simple tech problems.

Using the Five Computers as a Learning Center

Usually the five computers take up a concentrated space in the classroom and can easily be used in center rotations to:

- Research the topic on the Internet (check the school policies).
- Use CD-ROM dictionaries and encyclopedias.
- Use online dictionaries and encyclopedias (check the school policies).
- Use spreadsheets and databases to analyze information about the topic.
- Communicate the findings.
- Publish/post the results (check the school policies).
- Use content-specific software.
- Complete programmed instruction for content and skills.
- Gather information from a variety of sources (check the school policies).
- Participate in online discussions (check the school policies).
- Interview experts online (ask an expert) (check the school policies).
- Save all work for future use in a folder or on a disk.
- Practice needed skills.
- Use information gained in games.
- Write reports.
- Draw pictures, diagrams, and graphs, to accompany content.
- Create slides for a slide show or create a slide show.

Other Ways to Use the Five-Computer Classroom

If the computers are wireless laptops, they can be used in ways other than listed previously: Place students in small groups, one computer per group, to:

- Design a crossword puzzle.
- Write a portion of a never-ending story, passing their computer on to the next group after having written their paragraph.
- Play 20 Questions by sending questions to the teacher in a live chat.
- Complete online collaborative group projects.

Working in Classrooms with Individual Computers for Everyone

Some schools actually have provided or required one computer per child. In this situation, management of the equipment and technical troubleshooting become the issue rather than sharing resources. Teaching children to troubleshoot for themselves and treat the equipment with respect is a must. Ways to use computers when all students have one include

- Write in reflective journals daily and e-mail their responses to the teacher.
- Send e-mail messages to each other.
- Work on collaborative teams using online forums.

- Type work to be done.
- Find online content information.
- Do assignments on Blackboard or other online classroom environment.
- Complete WebQuests made of Word documents.

Keyboard Computers

Some schools save money by providing students with keyboard computers. These keyboards are designed to allow students to take notes, practice keyboarding, and store reports or essays without having to use a computer. The information can then be printed or transferred to central computers. These computers aren't able to run additional software and don't have very large memory capacity. Consider keeping the set of keyboard computers in a central location where they can be checked out individually or as a group. Students and teachers can use the keyboard computers in several ways:

- Take the computers to the library to do research.
- Type individual assignments.
- Take the computers on a field trip to take notes.
- Use the computers to record what happens during science experiments.

Handheld Computers (PDAs)

Another cost-effective way to provide every student a with computer is to use handheld computers or Personal Digital Assistants (PDAs). Handheld computers are a third the cost of a computer, yet allow students to use word processing, spreadsheets, databases, curriculum software, and some can even access the Internet and send e-mail. Handheld computers also allow for easy exchange of data. They have the ability to "beam" information to each other through an infrared port (which, of course, will need to be monitored closely). Use handheld computers to:

- Keep a calendar with assignment due dates.
- Sync to teacher's computer to pick up assignments for the day.
- Turn in assignments by beaming them to the teacher.
- Complete group assignments, each with an assigned part, sharing all information and turning in one paper.
- Document standards, benchmarks, and grades.

Collaborating with Technology Teachers in the Computer Lab

When you do not have computer access in the individual classrooms, many times there will be a computer lab in the building. To work effectively takes collaboration, communication, and coordination. Discover the purpose of the computer lab in the building. Is it to teach computer skills? Is it to complete programmed instruction? Is it to support individual teachers' classroom instruction? Does the classroom teacher have access to the lab or does a computer teacher staff it? If a computer teacher runs the lab, can classroom teachers collaborate to ensure instruction supports and benefits the standards and curriculum in the classroom? Is the lab staffed with "Gen www.Y" student mentors who can help you and your students?

Ways to use the computer lab include
- Instruct whole groups on keyboarding or other computer skills.
- Participate in individualized programmed instruction packages.
- Complete Accelerated Reader quizzes.
- Work on projects assigned by the classroom teacher.

Working with the Wireless Mobile Lab

A wireless mobile lab usually consists of a set of laptop computers housed in some sort of cart on wheels that allows the mobile lab to be wheeled into any classroom in the building. If the lab is used to connect to the Internet then a wireless access point may accompany the laptops. A wireless access point, plugged into the network connection in the classroom, acts as a network hub without wires. It emits radio signals that are picked up by wireless cards in the laptops similar to Ethernet cards. This allows the laptops to access the Internet, shared printers, and any other resources located on the school's network.

Wireless labs allow classroom teachers to use technology in their classrooms where they are comfortable and have access to their textbooks and other classroom resources or in places not usually considered, outside on the playground or on a field trip. Benefits include making every classroom a computer lab when needed, and making the Web accessible to students where wires are hard to string.

The mobile labs are very versatile. Use them as follows:
- Take the mobile lab to meetings where online information is reviewed.
- Use the mobile lab for staff technology training.
- Take the lab into the classroom for online searches.
- Take the mobile lab into the library so students can research and write.
- Take the mobile lab into the math classroom so everyone can use programs rather than seeing them demonstrated and having to try them later.
- Take the mobile lab into the language arts classroom so students can research and write under the supervision of the teacher.

Assistive Technology

Various technologies are used to support the living, working, and learning of people with disabilities. The Individuals with Disabilities Education Act (IDEA, available online at (http://www.ed.gov/offices/OSERS/IDEA/the_law.html)) defines assistive technology as "any item, piece of equipment, or product system, whether acquired commercially off the shelf, modified, or customized, that is used to increase, maintain, or improve functional capabilities of a child with disabilities". The assistive technology services required of IDEA include the evaluation of the needs of a child, purchasing, leasing, or otherwise providing for the acquisition of the device, adapting it to fit their needs, and training the child, family, and professionals to use the device(s). To see how assistive technology works, read Rian's story.

Rian's Story: Working and Learning Independently with Technology

The wonder of technology is how it can, by definition, make our daily tasks easier. For students with physical limitations and learning disabilities, the computer is a tool of independence and freedom from traditional restrictions.

Rian is a freshman in high school. He works out at a gym and swims three times a week. His friends are forming a band and he is learning to play the guitar with them. He likes people and is friendly to everyone. This year he is going to try drama and debate in addition to singing in the freshman boys' choir. He is looking forward to watching his friends play football and soccer at every home game. Rian has a part-time job and will work 5 to 10 hours a week, making sure to leave plenty of time for getting his homework done.

Rian is a typical high school freshman, except for the fact that he has mild cerebral palsy. How can a kid with a physical disability complicated by a reading disability accomplish school, extracurricular activities, and a job? Technology!

Rian uses **books on tape** to get information from textbooks. Many textbooks and other reading material are not available on tape so Rian uses a **pen scanner** to scan the text, upload it to a **computer**, and a **text reader** to read it back to him. Using the computer to compose writing assignments has allowed Rian to demonstrate more of his ability and less of his disability. Since he doesn't have to expend energy remembering how to form each letter, he can use that energy to compose thoughtful prose. Rian has the **Internet** available at school to conduct research. His **reader software** reads html pages to him and he can pick out valid information to copy and keep on **digital note cards**. He can also use **Excel** to create any graph he needs. Rian also uses his **online e-mail** account to transfer files to school and home so he doesn't have to carry a heavy backpack.

Rian is not using technology differently from other students his age. But the ability to use it regularly has leveled the playing field for him and allowed him to live, work, and learn independently.

Disabilities and Assistive Technology

IDEA defines several disabilities that might be noted in children. Those categories include mental retardation, hearing impairments, speech or language impairments, visual impairments, serious emotional disturbance, orthopedic impairments, autism, traumatic brain injury, other health impairments, and specific learning abilities. The disability categories more commonly found in schools are listed below with some assistive technology devices that allow students with varying abilities and disabilities the ability to perform daily activities at home and school.

Hearing Impairments
- amplification systems
- hearing aids
- signal systems
- telephones
- closed captioned video
- cochlear implants

Speech or Language Impairments
- touchboards
- computers
- word processing

Visual Impairments or Reading Disabilities
- word processing font size changes
- talking books
- scanning and reading software
- screen magnifiers
- screen readers
- Braille note takers
- speech synthesizer for instrument reading

Orthopedic Impairments
- braces, canes, crutches, walkers
- scooters, wheelchairs
- transfer boards, slings, belts
- stairlifts, lifts, vans
- special computer input devices
- speech recognition software
- exercise devices

Assistive Toys.
Assistive toys can be found that match the child's age, stage, and disability to a specific toy. See Dragonfly Toys at http://www.dragonflytoys.com/.

TECHNOLOGY TOOLS IN EDUCATIONAL SETTINGS

The ISTE NETS*T Standard 5 addresses the teacher's use of "technology to enhance their productivity and professional practice." The use of a variety of educational software in schools will address this standard. The **ISTE NETS*T Standard 3, Teaching, Learning, and the Curriculum**, and **ISTE NETS*T Standard 4, Assessment and Evaluation**, will require that you use the technology with students and also require them to use it.

Within the educational setting, tools for productivity and professional practice will likely include
- word processing
- spreadsheets and gradebook packages
- databases
- Internet and e-mail
- curriculum software
- CD-ROM encyclopedias
- digital imaging

Word Processing

Starting with the known, most preservice and practicing teachers use a computer for word processing. Word processing increases your productivity, takes less time, looks better than handwritten copy, checks your spelling, suggests a word, allows for a quick change of, or deletion of, words, phrases, paragraphs, or pages, and lets you save things for future use.

Beyond simple word processing for papers or reports, what else can teachers do with word processing programs?
- Write lesson plans.
- Write notes home to students or parents (use a cursive font to make it look more personal).
- File administrative and building reports.
- Create worksheets and assignments.
- Design posters or charts for classroom use (can be used as printed or enlarged with copy machine).
- Make a template to use for daily lesson plans or student assignments.
- Design rubrics for evaluation— specific lessons (insert an appropriate sized table and fill in the concepts, criteria, and grading scale).
- Prepare a classroom, unit, or school newsletter.
- Insert pictures into newsletters or use them for creative writing.
- Insert an Internet link into an assignment so that when the student uses the disk copy of the assignment, a click on the link connects them directly to the site needed, a simple and easy WebQuest. (http://edweb.sdsu.edu/courses/EDTEC596/About_WebQuests.html)

How can students use word processing?
- Learn keyboarding skills.
- Write reports, letters, or newsletters. Add pictures.
- Write spelling words (automatic spell check gives an immediate wrong or right).
- Insert pictures and/or photographs as story prompts.
- Categorize information in tables.
- Write a story. Link it to informational Internet sites.
- Take notes in class.
- Make a flowchart.
- Outline papers.
- Summarize information (AutoSummarize).
- Make labels for portfolios.
- Make posters, invitations, cards, charts, banners, signs, etc.
- Make pictures and collages.
- Annotate or edit writing easily.
- Read others' writing and edit or comment.
- Download reports and articles and highlight important pieces.

Spreadsheets

Most word processing packages come with a spreadsheet program. In its simplest form, it can be used to make a table to print and use to record attendance and grades. In its more advanced forms, it will actually calculate, average, and provide a statistical analysis of grades. However, student information is confidential and only you should have access to it. Be very cautious if the computer is not secured for teacher use only. (See further information on FERPA elsewhere in this book.)

What else can teachers do with spreadsheets?
- Prepare class rosters.
- Record attendance.
- Maintain student portfolio information.
- Calculate and record grades.
- Record benchmarks and assessments.
- Enter, compile, and manipulate simple data.
- Maintain classroom and departmental budgets.
- Create graphs and timelines.

How can students use spreadsheets?
- Alphabetize words or names.
- Calculate sums, differences, products, etc.
- Write vocabulary words and definitions. (Alphabetize over the year. Keep to study for standardized tests.)
- Keep track of assignments, due dates, possible grade, and actual grade.
- Keep track of books read by title, author, type, and interest level.
- Make a flowchart.

- Compare information in various types of graphs.
- Keep scientific data from experiments.
- Keep track of car expenses (payment [interest and principal], insurance, maintenance [gas, oil, car washes], minor repairs, major repairs).
- Maintain a class bank, or individual bank accounts for purposes of behavior management.
- Record the weather over time. Chart. Graph.
- Record how a 24-hour weekday time is spent vs. how a 24-hour weekend day is spent. Graph and compare graphs.
- Monitor how allowances are spent.

Databases

Databases are less often used and their direct application to classroom practice may be most misunderstood. We might use a database at home to keep our address books current and our mailing lists updated. In fact, if you don't already, it is a good place to start. That concept can be taken directly into the classroom. Each year, you can enter student information into a database. Remember that confidential information needs to be housed on a secure computer. A database does allow you easy access to phone numbers and other emergency information. On a larger scale, the schools often have a student warehouse (database) of information to which teachers might or might not have access. Some of our technology leaders say, "A database is one of the computer tools that students should be able to use by the end of elementary school" (Heine, 1994, p. 39).

How can teachers use databases?
- Maintain information— enter student class information, e.g., name, grades, interests, age, birth dates, zip codes, test dates and results, etc.
- Sort and classify the information alphabetically or numerically to find those with like interests, similar birth dates, same ages.
- Search for information within the database.
- Archive information for your teaching portfolio or for student portfolios
- Merge any of this information into personalized letters or mailing labels.

How can students use databases?
- Make address book entries for family, friends, and classmates (check school policies before entering student data).
- Catalog CDs, video games, or videos.
- Catalog any collectibles with date and estimated cost.

Using the Internet for Research and Instruction

The Internet provides information at your fingertips that in the past might have taken days or weeks to locate. From a teacher's personal use perspective, it is most often used for purposes of research, locating and documenting information and communication (online discussion, listservs, threaded discussion boards, sending and receiving e-mail).

How can teachers use the information found on the Internet?
- Locate information about a school district.
- Read information from the professional association compatible with your teaching responsibilities.
- Look for jobs.
- Search for lesson plans. (See a listing of sites elsewhere in this book.
- Locate software. Many companies have free downloadable trials.
- Locate software reviews. Teachers don't have a lot of time to actually review software, but companies and professionals post their reviews.
- Find content information. (See a listing of sites by content area elsewhere in this book.)
- Instantly publish information.
- Locate virtual field trips.
- Locate WebQuests for a subject and grade level.
- Design and post virtual field trips.
- Design and post WebQuests for subject and grade level.
- Learn about technology tools through online instruction.
- Take online courses.
- Gain additional certifications through online programs.
- Teach online courses using educational courseware.
- Submit attendance and grade information through Web-based student information systems.

How can teachers use the Internet with students for research and other learning?
- **Check the school's Internet safe-use policies.**
- Establish online testing and data collection points.
- Have students complete WebQuests.
- Have students develop WebQuests to teach other students.
- Complete Internet searches.
- Post grades within educational courseware.
- Take online courses.
- Use Internet pictures of the day to bring curriculum alive, and as story starters for daily journal writing. (Try history, astronomy, or news.)
- Monitor the weather.
- Read the local, state, national, and international news.

Using the Internet for Communication

E-mail is but one of several forms of online two-way communication. Other forms include instant messaging (two people at a time), online chat (a group of people), and threaded discussion boards (a group of people talking asynchronously, usually about a given topic). Each can be used in unique ways in the classroom. (The laws associated with this are discussed elsewhere in this book.) Be sure to check district policies associated with online communication before using any form of it with students.

All forms of online communication can be used by teachers for personal information and/or productivity as well as used with students. How can teachers use the Internet for communication?
- Collaborate with other teachers.
- Participate in professional listservs, online chats, and/or threaded discussion groups.
- Send instant messages to resource teachers regarding the behavior of special needs students.
- Send and receive e-mails from colleagues.
- Send notes to colleagues and parents.
- Attach pictures and documents to e-mails.
- Send e-mail messages to students.

How can teachers use Internet communication tools for instruction? (**Check the school's Internet safe-use policies.**)
- Have students send e-mails to other students in the building. Set up e-pals with classes in other parts of the country.
- Collaborate with students in other parts of the country on weather, animal, or bird sighting projects. (Check school's e-mail policies.)

Using Instant Messaging in the Classroom

Instant messaging allows you to communicate immediately with others through online word processing where messages are sent instantly and replies typed and returned in a matter of seconds. Several tools are available: Yahoo, AIM, ICQ, and AOL. Teachers can keep in touch with one another before and after school and between classes. A tool such as this is invaluable when teachers share difficult students.
- Use Instant Messaging to be available for homework help or parental communication during virtual "office hours."
- Use Instant Messaging or online chat to bring in a virtual guest speaker.

Classroom Projects Using Instant Messaging

Students of all ages seem to really get involved in classroom projects using instant messaging. Some businesses are requiring employees to interact with each other in this way to collaborate on projects. The activity works well in either a computer lab or in a classroom where each student has access to a computer.

- Arrange students into groups of 4–5, but do not let them sit near each other.
- Assign them the task of completing a project, using instant messaging communication only.
- Take points off if you hear any talking or see anyone motioning or communicating in any other way.
- Discuss the pros and cons of communicating in this fashion. Share ways the students compensated for visual and body clues.
- If possible, compare this to a similar lesson in which group work was done in a face-to-face manner.
- Think about how this method could be used for long-term projects, perhaps allowing some oral communication.

Classroom Projects Using Threaded Discussion
Complete a lesson using a threaded discussion board instead of real time messaging. Discuss the differences between person-to-person collaboration, instant messaging, and threaded discussion. Does it help to have time to think about your responses? Does threading the conversation help to keep track of what you're talking about versus the linear way an instant messaging conversation takes place? Which do you like best? Why? Which do you like least? Why?

Online Chats
Host a "Saturday morning cartoon alternative" as a club, for a class on an academic topic, or just for fun.

- Meet online from 8 to 9 a.m. on Saturday morning with a preselected topic.
- Invite a guest speaker if possible.
- Hold a one-hour virtual chat.
- Provide the log of the chat online and continue the discussion through the week using a threaded discussion board.
- Parents, administrators, or other teachers could be invited to participate.

Collaborative Workspace
Collaborative or shared workspaces on a network are files or folders that more than one person can access. Another way to think of a collaborative space is to think of the group of people who might use it. It could be a group of students working on a project together. It could be the teacher and students of one class. To help them collaborate, all members of a group have access to the same files and folders. Each member of the group can use this space to share work and information with the others.

Collaborative workspaces can also include communication areas such as online chat or threaded discussion boards. There are other options such as drawing spaces, shared photo albums, shared browsers for collaborative Web browsing, and more. Many companies are offering free collaborate workspace online.

Microsoft Office XP features SharePoint Team ServicesTM that allow users to collaborate on documents and collect information over the Internet or local network.

Links Related to Collaborative Work Spaces
Groove.net
  http://groove.net/
iTeamWork.com
  http://www.iteamwork.com/
Learning Circuits
  http://www.learningcircuits.com/aug2000/digenti.html
Yahoo Groups
  http://groups.yahoo.com/
Groups@AOL
  http://dynamic.aol.com/cgi/redircomplex?url=http://groups.aol.com&sid=pGp
Microsoft SharePoint Team ServicesTM
  http://www.microsoft.com/frontpage/sharepoint

Graphics, Animation, and Multimedia

Pictures, sounds, and movies are a very important part of our everyday communication. It is important that we know how and when to use these tools in the classroom. For many years teachers have been using filmstrips and pictures to help students visualize concepts and to gain exposure to things that they haven't seen before. We have upgraded these tools to include videotape, laserdiscs, and movies, photos, and sound bites available on the Internet. We also have the tools to create our own multimedia teaching tools. PowerPoint is a popular presentation tool that allows teachers to create multimedia instruction. Words can be enhanced by graphics, movies, and sounds put together in a complete presentation with transitions. With a digital camera, teachers can document field trips, classroom activities, student work, and share these on classroom Web pages, PowerPoint Presentations, as an e-mail attachments and in print. Desktop Digital Video tools like iMovie allow teachers to emphasize and enhance a lesson using the communication students are accustomed to. Teaching students the ability to conceive, produce, and edit meaningful video sequences moves out of the domain of the specialist and becomes an important basic communications skill.

How else can teachers use graphics and multimedia?
• Share different cultures with sound bites and photos on the Internet.
• Personalize nametags with photos.
• Create individualized flashcards and handouts.
• Create instructional video.
• Create online instruction for distance education.
• Create virtual field trips.

How can students use graphics and multimedia?
- Enhance reports, stories, and poetry.
- Share information on the Internet or in e-mail.
- Create visual demonstrations.
- Create interactive communication.
- Create virtual field trips.

Digital Imaging Technology

Image processing can be used to enhance images as well as to extract information from images. Graphics are pictures or visual representations of an object. If we look at every individual pixel of an image, we can process much meaningful information about that object. Image analysis in the classroom can be used to promote inquiry in achieving science, geography, art, and mathematics goals.

Many students are visual learners and the representation of equations by graphing takes them one step closer to understanding. Take that visual representation another step by putting the axis into a picture of a brain or a satellite image taken of Earth, and you now have a meaningful image to measure, extract data from, and make genuine inquiries about. Students can learn how to process and analyze digital images from the fields of medicine, cell biology, genetics, biotechnology, neuroimaging, and more. They can also learn how to enhance images to bring out important features, make precise measurements from digital images, manipulate and analyze PET and MRI data, and animate time-lapse and 3-D data.

Digital images can be used in many ways:
- Use digital images for classroom instruction.
- Post digital images to the Internet.
- Share digital images among students
- Gather digital images into digital portfolios.
- Analyze digital images with simple but sophisticated software developed at the National Institute of Health.

More information about using digital imaging in the math and science content areas can be found elsewhere in this book.

References

Heine, E. (1994). The world at their fingertips. *The Florida Technology in Education Quarterly, 7*(1), 38-42.

Roblyer, M. D., & Edwards, J. (2000). *Integrating educational technology into teaching.* Upper Saddle River, NJ: Merrill/Prentice Hall.

Wilder, R., & Gebhardt, M. (2001). *Creating templates for term papers and labs.* Educator's Guide to Computers in the Classroom 2(3), 11–14.

USING THE INTERNET FOR INSTRUCTION: CRITICAL ISSUES

The Internet is an enormous information highway that we encounter on our travels. I [Jeri] can remember clearly my first experience with the Internet. In a summer course, little more than 3–4 years ago, I asked students to bring in an Internet site related to advice for parents about child-rearing (infants, toddlers, preschoolers, elementary-aged students, preadolescents, adolescents, or young adults). They came in the next day with Web sites they had chosen. We had gathered more information in 24 hours than I had ever imagined possible. Interestingly, I didn't even know how to get on the Internet. The students excited me so that I had to try it for myself. That afternoon I headed to the lab for some one-on-one instruction. The class compiled a list of the sites and addresses (I now know to call them URLs). They organized the Web sites by age level (if only I had known about spreadsheets or databases at the time) and made copies for everyone (could have posted them on a Web site).

Tonya has helped Jeri learn a lot more about the Internet. To use the Internet one needs a computer with an Internet connection and a browser. A browser is software that allows us to view the information coming in from the Internet. Netscape and Microsoft's Internet Explorer are the most popular browsers, but there are several others. In addition to a browser, there are plug-ins (extra software) that are necessary to view some multimedia and other files. Usually plug-ins are available as a free download. Some are becoming so popular that they are being added as a permanent feature in newer versions of Netscape and Internet Explorer. Adobe Acrobat Reader is used to view portable document format (PDF) files. Macromedia Shockwave and Macromedia Flash are used to access animation and sound. Real Player is used to access streaming video and music. Apple's QuickTime and Window's Media Player are used to access movies and other multimedia.

Social, Ethical, Legal, and Human Issues Related to Internet Use

Just as with books, magazines, and libraries, not all information on the Internet is top quality nor is it appropriate for student use. With the recent implementation of several US laws, some legal protections are provided. It is still up to teachers and parents to monitor what is retrieved, to teach students how to determine the quality and appropriateness of the material, and to report any violations when material and/or requests are not appropriate.

The **ISTE NETS*T Standard 6** relates to social, ethical, legal and human issues surrounding the use of technology. The **ISTE NETS*S Standard 2** addresses social, ethical, and human issues. In this section of our book, we address many of the social, ethical, legal, and human issues related to technology use and to promoting safe and healthy use of technology resources.

25

Laws Related to Internet Use

Several recent US laws now govern our use of the Internet: *Children's Online Privacy Protection Act* (COPPA), *Children's Internet Protection Act* (CIPA), *Family Educational Rights and Privacy Act* (FERPA). In addition, laws addressing copyright have been extended to technology sources. Although many of these laws are being contested based on the First Amendment right of free speech— **It is critical to check school policies related to COPPA, CIPA, and FERPA.**

Children's Online Privacy Protection Act (COPPA)

The Children's Online Privacy Protection Act (COPPA), which went into effect April 21, 2000, affects US commercial Web sites and third-party commercial Web sites that schools permit their students to access. COPPA requires "operators of websites or online services directed to children and operators of websites or online services who have actual knowledge that the person from whom they seek information is a child (1) to post prominent links on their websites to a notice of how they collect, use, and/or disclose personal information from children; (2) with certain exceptions, to notify parents that they wish to collect information from their children and obtain parental consent prior to collecting, using, and/or disclosing such information; (3) not to condition a child's participation in online activities on the provision of more personal information than is reasonably necessary to participate in the activity; (4) to allow parents the opportunity to review and/or have their children's information deleted from the operator's database and to prohibit further collection from the child; and (5) to establish procedures to protect the confidentiality, security, and integrity of personal information they collect from children." As directed by COPPA, the act also provides a safe harbor for operators following Commission-approved, self-regulatory guidelines. (The Children's Online Privacy Protection Act document can is available on the US Federal Trade Commission website, at http://www.ftc.gov/os/1999/9910/64fr59888.htm.)

Nonprofit sites are not included in the act; however, many are voluntarily complying. A key component of COPPA is that sites must have a privacy policy disclosing what information is being collected, how it is being used, and with whom they will share the information. A second component requires that when personal information (name, address, phone, and e-mail address) is collected from a child under thirteen, parents must be informed and their consent given. The third component deals with Internet safety. **Children under thirteen must have parental consent to use communication technologies prior to use** (chat, e-mail, instant messaging, e-pals, discussion boards, video conferencing, etc.).

Children's Internet Protection Act (CIPA)

The Children's Internet Protection Act (CIPA) went into effect April 20, 2001, requiring that schools and libraries that receive certain types of federal technology funding have safe-use Internet policies. The policies require the use of Internet filtering software to screen material that is inappropriate (obscene) or harmful to minors and the monitoring of student Internet use. Free speech challenges to this law have been made with regard to libraries, but none yet on the CIPA requirements for schools. Schools and libraries must begin addressing the provisions in the law July 1, 2001, indicating whether they have complied, are in the process of complying, will be compliant by the next year, or need not comply (http://www.neirls.org/consulting/lawfilter.htm).

Family Educational Rights and Privacy Act (FERPA)

The Family Educational Rights and Privacy Act (FERPA) protects the privacy of student education records and applies to all schools that receive funds under an applicable program of the US Department of Education. FERPA gives parents certain rights with respect to their children's education records and the rights transfer to the student at 18 or when they attend a school beyond the high school level. Schools must notify parents and eligible students annually of their rights under FERPA. Those rights include

- Parents or eligible students have the right to inspect and review the student's education records maintained by the school.
- Parents or eligible students have the right to request that a school correct the records, which they believe to be inaccurate or misleading.
- Generally, schools must have written permission from the parent or eligible student in order to release any information from a student's education record and parents have a right to deny that release.
- (http://www.ed.gov/offices/OM/fpco/ferpa1.html)

Personally identifiable information includes the student's name, address, Social Security number, or any other information that makes the student's identity easily traceable (http://www.ed.gov/offices/OM/fpco/ferparegs.html). **Teachers must be cautious about posting student work or student information online as well as being cautious about the use of electronic communication.**

Copyright and Fair Use

Copyright protects authors of "original works of authorship," including literary, dramatic, musical, artistic, and certain other intellectual works. This protection gives the owner of copyright the exclusive right to, and to authorize others to, reproduce the work, prepare derivative works, distribute copies, perform the work, display the work, and in the case of sound recordings, to perform the work by means of digital audio transmission. **The penalties for infringement are very harsh.** "It is illegal for anyone to violate any of the rights provided by the copyright law to the owner of copyright. . . . In some cases, these limitations are specified exemptions from copyright liability. One major limitation is the doctrine of 'fair use'" (http://www.loc.gov/copyright/circs/circ1.html#wci). However, determining fair use is sometimes difficult. A comprehensive set of links associated with copyright and fair use resources on the Internet appears at http://groton.k12.ct.us/mts/pt2a.htm.

A Further Word of Caution

Remember, information on the Internet is not just available and or published in the US. Our laws do not cover everything that is on the Internet. Because of this, parents and teachers must be responsible in what they require of students to see that they are protected online.

Social, Ethical, and Human Issues Related to Internet Use

Beyond the legal issues, there are other social, ethical, and human issues related to Internet use. These include the digital divide and social etiquette.

Digital Divide

Within any classroom, there are students who have more than others— money, intelligence, or material goods. In addition, there "has always been a gap between those people and communities who can make effective use of information technology and those who cannot. Now, more than ever, unequal adoption of technology excludes many from reaping the fruits of the economy." "Digital divide" refers to the gap between those who can effectively use new information and communication tools, such as the Internet, and those who cannot (http://www.digitaldividenetwork.org/content/sections/index.cfm?key=2).

Some solutions to the digital divide in the news worldwide recently include
- E-branch libraries (library kiosks placed in schools, grocery stores, and malls), which provide patrons with computers and phone-line Internet access to libraries.
  http://www.digitaldividenetwork.org/content/news/index.cfm?key=413
- The distribution of at least 100,000 high-capacity computer game consoles equipped with satellite links to schools and in homes in Third World countries.
  http://www.digitaldividenetwork.org/content/news/index.cfm?key=412
- European Union telecoms ministers backing a proposal "to bring the Internet to every citizen's house." The plan, which would update existing so-called universal service provisions for access to voice telephony and fax lines, requires operators to guarantee "functional Internet access even in unprofitable regions, such as remote geographical areas."
  http://www.digitaldividenetwork.org/content/news/index.cfm?key=395.

For further information on the digital divide, see these two Web sites dedicated to information on the digital divide:
- *Closing the Digital Divide*
  http://www.digitaldivide.gov/
- *Digital Divide Network*
- http://www.digitaldividenetwork.org/content/sections/index.cfm

Assessing and Addressing the Digital Divide in Classrooms

In order to give assignments that students can complete, it is necessary to find out what technology students have access to at home, in public places, at boys' and girls' clubs, at friends' and relatives' homes, etc. Having students help you develop a list of all the **technologies** they can think of to place in one column and providing several columns for **use** (home, library, school, relative, other) will let you know the extent of the digital divide in your class of students. Seeking appropriate accommodations to include all students in the activities of the classroom is a responsibility all teachers have. (Source: Michael Jordon and Gib Stuve at the ISTE NETS for Teachers Writing Session, held in Wheeling, WV, August 2000)

Netiquette
As students use the Internet for communication, rules of etiquette need to be examined. Network etiquette (Netiquette) is "a set of rules for behaving properly online" (Virginia Shea, 1994, 2000, online at http://www.albion.com/netiquette). Shea's core rules include

- Remember the human. (Never forget that the person reading your mail or posting is, indeed, a person, with feelings that can be hurt.)
- Adhere to the same standards of behavior online that you follow in real life. (Be ethical and don't break the law.)
- Know where you are in cyberspace. (Netiquette varies from domain to domain, personal to professional, business to education, etc.)
- Respect other people's time and bandwidth. (Be brief, to the point, and considerate.)

Traveling the Super Highway with Students: Addressing Social, Legal, Ethical, and Human Issues Online

For some time, the Internet has been referred to as a superhighway. As in real life, hackers, trespassers, and robbers play their havoc as one travels the superhighway. Advice to world travelers often includes words of wisdom such as "Don't go into dark alleys," "Stick with the group," and "Be wary of strangers." These words of wisdom, along with others, are chosen to outline the legal and ethical issues associated with Internet use.

Obtaining a Passport: School Internet Use Policies
To protect students online is both a legal and ethical issue. Remember to do these things before traveling with students.

- Locate the school's Internet safe-use policies and make sure parents have given students permission to use the Internet.
- Preview the Internet sites you want your students to use.
- Post a set of safe sites (like visas to visit other countries) on your Web site.
- If you search for sites on your home computers, remember to try them on the school computers. Schools and/or districts, to lock out inappropriate information for students, are establishing firewalls. It could be that, for some reason, filtering software will lock out the site you chose at home.

Reporting Suspected Intruders: Stranger Danger

As with real-life strangers, students need to be wary of child predators on the Internet and be instructed to report any unwanted, uncomfortable, and/or unsolicited approaches by strangers. Recent legislation indicates how serious our government is about the protection of children online. **COPPA and CIPA** provide guidelines and consequences for protecting children online. No one can ask students under 13 to report inappropriate information to them. That doesn't mean that it won't happen. It just means that it is against the law to do so.

- Train students in what their rights online are. No one online is to ask them for identifying information and they are not to give it without their parent's consent.
- Remind students to report when they think someone has requested any information from them— "think" is the key word here, just as "suspected" child abuse must be reported.
- Students should not have to confirm that information has been solicited. It will be up to others to determine that incident. Suspicion is enough to warrant a report to you.
- As with all infractions of the law, students need to be encouraged to report their findings to the proper authorities and feel comfortable doing so.

Minding and Establishing Road Blocks

When traveling, we sometimes run into roadblocks which have been put there for our protection. Do we move the barricades or do we take the detour? The same is true for the Super Highway. Often a notice will appear that you are leaving or entering a secure site.

- Teach students about roadblocks— They are there for student protection.
- Teach students what to do about roadblocks— Do Not Enter!
- If students come upon a sign telling them they are leaving a safe site, ask them to seek permission from you to leave the site, and then monitor the next sites closely to see what is outside the protected site.

When traveling, we often take the wrong road and end up at places we didn't want to go. Or we might find a fallen rock that impedes travel. When that happens, we often give future travelers a cautionary word and/or report the problem to the authorities. **CIPA** will require the use of filtering software, but until firewalls are in place, it is the teacher's responsibility to monitor students. Offensive or unsafe Internet sites can be entered by accident when we have no intention of going there. The simple, innocent mistake of using the wrong domain designator (.com rather than .edu) can place us in embarrassing situations. The same can happen with our students.

To help students learn what to do when these things happen

- Teach students what to do when accidents occur or potential accidents are about to happen--Report accidents to proper authorities!

- Warn the next groups who travel the paths leading to this unsavory site to be cautious. (Remember, too, that just telling students about issues like this might only arouse their curiosity.)

Assuring Private Housing

When traveling, we look for secure and safe housing. Safety and privacy also need to be considered on the Internet. Secure files, secure computers, secure information all seem to be targets for those "highwaymen" who see hacking as creative thinking and problem-solving activities. The **Family Education Rights and Protection Act (FERPA)** guarantees students and families privacy. Each district has a policy designed to require its employees to be in line with this Act. All teachers need to know and follow these policies. Typically,

- Know and follow district policies related to FERPA.
- Grades should not be reported or accessible to anyone except appropriate school personnel and family members.
- Grades can be safely posted within courseware.
- Every effort should be made to keep confidential information confidential.
- Online publishing of student work should contain no identifying information other than first name, the school, and in some instances, the grade level.

Avoiding Highway Robbery

Robbery occurs in society, along the information highway, and in schools. Copyrighted information entered the school place, first with textbooks, and more recently with software and technology tools. As it became easier and easier to do, copying of copyrighted information occurred more frequently. Often the perpetrator did so with good intent to share something exciting with a colleague, to allow more students to use an exciting product, or to make sure that they had a copy if things got lost/stolen. However, the copyright is there to protect the author and publisher and the long hours, time, and expense they put into the product. Recent litigation reported in the national news shows the severity of these highway robberies and the potential losses of revenue for many different companies.

Teachers and students alike should understand issues associated with "fair use".
- Students must be taught **copyright and fair use** policies.
- Warn students against copying information for which there is a copyright.
- Students can use the information from Internet sites just the same as they can use information from books, magazines, journals, etc. Rather than "stealing" it from someone else, teach students how to identify the use of this information appropriately rather than plagiarizing it.
- Teach students how to ask permission to use information, graphics, icons, etc. A request can be sent to the author or organization describing the desired use and seeking permission.

- When identifying information is not available and when there is no copyright, citing the source of the information is critical. Using the URL and the date of acquisition provide a legitimate documentation.
- In teacher education you may need to cite electronic sources. See APA Style: Electronic Resources http://www.apastyle.org/elecref.html

Protecting Your Valuables

Many software and technology tools allow a backup file to protect the originals. In schools this could translate to a library of originals and copies kept in separate CD notebooks, with copies being checked out for use and originals kept secure. To then keep the copies secure—

- Program/software can be installed on classroom computers using the copy while the original is kept secure and away from those who might want to copy it. Once installed, the teacher using the copy should keep it in his/her possession so that only legitimate copies are in use.
- When use is completed, the software/tool should be removed from the hard drive, and the copy returned to the CD library.
- When a legitimate copy is available in the school library of software, the program can be used.

Writing Home

In mail delivery, we have come a long way since the Pony Express, mail trains, airmail, and overnight delivery of letters. Now, instantly, colleagues around the world can converse, collaborate, and work together in many ways. Remember:

- Children under 13 must have parental consent to use communication technologies (chat, e-mail, instant messaging, e-pals, discussion boards, video conferencing, etc.), prior to use (Children's Online Privacy Protection Act [COPPA]).
- It is good to inform or seek permission from parents of other students also.
- Children must be taught the social graces of online communication.

Using Internet Etiquette

The Internet as a communication tool is a lot faster than the Pony Express of old. Messages and responses are delivered around the world in a matter of minutes, rather than days, weeks, or months. However, Internet etiquette (Netiquette), still exists.

- Begin "letters" with name, an address, a date (most times done automatically to the minute), a topic, a salutation, a knowledge of the reader, a clear note, expectations, and a closing.
- Rather than weighing the pony down with unwanted mail and possible illness, one should avoid passing on junk mail, chain letters, and viruses. Check those chain letters. Although not necessarily illegal on the Internet, they can consume an enormous amount of time and space.

EVALUATING AND USING WEB SITES

Verifying Information We Encounter on the Internet

When we plan to go on a trip, we have to be careful of the people we deal with, especially when we go to places we have not been before. Taking an eTrip and traveling the superhighway are the same. We can encounter wonderful information. However, we can also encounter false information. With written print, some categorization occurs— fiction, nonfiction, verification of copyright, registration, ISBN numbers. With online information, very little validation of the information presently occurs in any organized fashion. It is often left up to the "traveler" to verify the information.

In order to make any sense of information we are constantly barraged with, we must all learn to be critical information consumers. Although COPPA, CIPA, FERPA, and copyright laws provide protection for students and families, not all information on the Internet is quality information, or appropriate for use with students. To monitor that information, teachers and parents must evaluate Web sites for their appropriateness.

- Learn how to evaluate a Web site.
- Evaluate Web sites for personal use and for use in instruction.
- Teach students how to evaluate Web sites.

Evaluating Web sites has several components for the average person traveling the Internet and additional ones for teachers who suggest sites for their students. In order to use sites on the Web, we must ask ourselves questions about content, authenticity, learning strategies, navigation, graphics, appeal, and availability.

Content

- Is the reading level appropriate for your students?
- Is the type of information appropriate for your students?
- Is the information comprehensive?
- Is the information biased?
- Does the information support your curriculum objectives?
- Will the content address student outcomes?
- Is the information accurate?
- Is the information organized so that your students can use it?

Authenticity

- What is the source of the information?
- What is the date of the most recent update?
- What is the intent of the authors?
- Is the information objective or subjective, factual or opinion?
- Can the facts be verified by another source? If not, what is the reason?
- Is the author's contact information available?
- What citations are provided within the site?

Learning Strategies
- What levels of learning are addressed?
- Which of the multiple intelligences are addressed?
- What is required of the students?
- Does it require active or passive learning?
- Will this site challenge your students appropriately?

Navigation
- Is the page well organized? Could your students easily navigate the site?
- Are there advertisements?
- Are there pop-up windows? If so, are they appropriate?
- What links are located in the site and where do they take you?
- Does it have a searchable index?
- Are software plug-ins necessary to view the site?
- Can you get around in the site quickly and efficiently?
- How much time will students spend at this site?

Graphics
- Are the graphics appropriate for your students?
- Do the graphics add to or distract from the information?
- Do the graphics delay the loading of the site?

Appeal
- Does it look good? Is it appealing?
- Is there a good balance of graphics and information?

Availability
- Is the site readily available or frequently down?
- If the site has changed URLs, does the automatic roll over to the new address occur? If not, is the new address entry given?

Preselecting Sites and Designing a Map

When the traveler is a veteran, it is easy to travel to places. When the traveler is a novice, it is more difficult, and they may be advised to follow a map. Young children tend to believe everything they see and hear and must be cautioned about doing so on the Internet. To help students avoid inappropriate sites as outlined by **CIPA,** teachers need to
- Select the sites to visit and monitor the credibility of the sites.
- In a word processing document, type the names, URLs and a brief description of three or four sites. Have students select one of these to examine. Or take short site-seeing trips to all three or four Internet sites to determine where they might like to spend more time.
- Locate locked sites, closed gates, and/or warnings that one is entering unmonitored territory.
- Design WebQuests (maps). WebQuests provide a map to follow, one way for preselected sites to be connected to the curriculum.

WebQuests

A WebQuest is a collection of Web sites that are linked to a specific written question, task, or story. They link your curriculum and standards together while using technology as a tool to enhance and engage your students. WebQuests provide responsible classroom use of the Internet in the form of a Web page or hyperlinked word document with curriculum-based challenges and timely resources. Teachers preselect Web sites on a topic and create an inquiry-based activity using this information, connecting it to information from textbooks or other sources. Teachers can limit students' search time and, at the same time, keep students safe by having them view only what the teachers want them to view, and connecting their classroom tasks with the materials provided.

WebQuests can be written to encourage many thinking skills such as:
- Comparing and contrasting
- Inducing and deducing
- Analyzing or classifying
- Problem solving and decision making
- Critical and creative thinking

Learning About WebQuests
The first step to creating your own WebQuest is to examine some created by other teachers to learn about what they are and how they work. The first site listed here is designed for younger students. The second is for older students.
- *An Insect's Perspective* http://projects.edtech.sandi.net/grant/insects/
- *Land of the Free and Home of the Braves*
  http://www.lfelem.lfc.edu/tech/DuBose/webquest/miller/amerishame.html

Locating WebQuests
Several WebQuest collections are noted in the Online Resource section of this book. Two of our favorites are
- *The WebQuest Page* (Dodge) http://edweb.sdsu.edu/webquest/webquest.html
- *TrackStar* http://trackstar.hprtec.org/

Creating Your Own WebQuest
Once you have decided that you can use WebQuests with your students, follow these steps to create your own.
- **Determine the content.** Usually teachers look at a lesson in the text (for example, "safety") or select a specific content standard (for example, apply a decision-making process to health issues and problems).
- **Search for sites.** Use your favorite search engine for the age group of your students. Type in a general term (safety) or a more specific term (fire safety education). Visit several sites to see which are most appealing to you and best fit the needs of your students. (See the section on Evaluating Web Sites, located elsewhere in this book.) This is probably the most time- consuming

part for the teacher, but allows the students to spend their time reading, researching, and responding instead of searching.

- **Select your favorite links.** Once you have zeroed in on a few sites, and even though you think they may fit your needs, take a thorough trip into, in, and around the site. If there are links to other sites, follow the links— as many as 3-4 links deep— to see where your students might go if your guard is down. If you are to leave the safe site, you may find a warning posted. You will find that to keep students safe, some sites are locked and once you are in them you can't get out.

- **Build the lesson.** How are you going to present this information to your students? Will it come before the text material as a motivational activity? Will it be a part of the research? Will it allow students to compare and contrast the information from the text with information from the Internet? What content standards and district benchmarks do you want it to meet?

- **Use an online WebQuest generator.** WebQuest generators allow you to write the content of the WebQuest and create an online document without having to know anything about hyperlinks, Web pages, or Web servers. They allow you to input your specific questions and your preselected and previewed Web sites and then create the WebQuest for you. Two online WebQuest generators are

  - *TrackStar* http://trackstar.hprtec.org/
  - *Filamentality* http://www.kn.pacbell.com/wired/fil/

- **Design Your Own Format.** WebQuests can be written and printed out for students to use with the URLs given for the students to type in. One letter typed incorrectly can cause lots of frustration. WebQuests can also be created using an electronic version of a Word document.

  - Just as if you were telling your students some new information, write an instructional story, providing students with the details.
  - When there are spots in your storytelling that have sites linked to them, put the URL in parentheses. Word will automatically create a hyperlink for URLs. If the student is online while viewing the Word document and clicks on the URL, they will automatically be taken to that Web site.
  - It is also possible in Word to hide the URL behind the printed words or pictures.
    - Highlight the words or pictures you want linked.
    - Under "Insert" go to "hyperlink."
    - Enter the URL into the box labeled "Link to File or URL."
    - When you return to the Word document, the words themselves are linked and most often will have turned blue and are underlined.
  - WebQuests can also be created as a Web page. The Web page can be used locally from the classroom computer or can be uploaded to a Web server and made available on the Internet. A template to develop a WebQuest as a Web page is located at http://edweb.sdsu.edu/webquest/LessonTemplate.html.

INTEGRATING ISTE STANDARDS INTO
ENGLISH LANGUAGE ARTS

The **National Council of Teachers of English (NCTE),** an organization primarily of and for teachers, is devoted to improving the teaching and learning of English and the language arts at all levels of education (*http://www.ncte.org/about/*). Their mission is to promote "the development of literacy, the use of language to construct personal and public worlds and to achieve full participation in society, through the learning and teaching of English and the related arts and sciences of language." The **International Reading Association (IRA)** has a professional membership of classroom teachers, reading specialists, consultants, administrators, supervisors, university faculty, researchers, psychologists, librarians, media specialists, and parents. It is dedicated to "promoting high levels of literacy for all by improving the quality of reading instruction, disseminating research and information about reading, and encouraging the lifetime reading habit." NCTE and IRA worked to establish the student Standards for English/Language Arts. Their goals include professional development, advocacy, partnerships, research, and global literacy development (http://www.reading.org/about/).

The ELA standards, published elsewhere in this book, are used in accreditation processes in many states and are approved by the National Council for the Accreditation of Teacher Education (NCATE) that provides a voluntary accreditation for over 2,000 colleges of education in the United States (http://www.ncate.org/).

Several of the 12 standards provide specific references to technology and can be addressed by activities provided within this section:
- Standard 1 addresses the student use of print and non-print texts to understand themselves and others and to gather new information.
- Standard 3 addresses students interacting with other readers and writers.
- Standard 6 addresses students applying their knowledge of media techniques (among others) to create, critique, and discuss print and non-print texts.
- Standard 7 addresses students conducting research, gathering information from a variety of resources (print and non-print).
- Standard 8 addresses students using a variety of technological and information resources (e.g., libraries, databases, computer networks, video) to gather, synthesize, create, and communicate knowledge.

The **ISTE NETS for Student Standards** that most align with the ELA area include Standard 3, Technology Productivity Tools, Standard 4, Technology Communications Tools, and Standard 5, Technology Research Tools.

Technology Tools for English/Language Arts

Word Processing for Adults

Each of us has our favorite word processing programs, but two commonly used programs are Microsoft Word and Corel WordPerfect. Both are easily used with Macintosh and Windows operating systems for word processing, creating, and editing text documents. Both have options to save documents as standard text (several fonts and sizes), HTML (for Web delivery), and RTF (rich text format a universal file type, compatible with other operating systems and software), etc. Both also include desktop publishing features and usually come in a package with spreadsheet and database programs, allowing comprehensive presentation and communication of information. The programs come with built-in "help" menus, and several online tutorials are available and easily located. Use your favorite search engine, type in the name of the program followed by "tutorial."

Word Processing for PreK–12 Students

In their simplest way, young children begin their written communication with scribbles, pictures, attempts at written letter and word production, and eventually write in a more "adult" way. Our favorite tool that supports the emergence of oral and written language is Kid Pix. Kid Pix is a comprehensive program that can actually be used by students of all ages, but fits well with young children. It allows one to write, draw, and paint; input video, pictures, and sound; and create multimedia presentations with animation and sound features. It allows children to: (a) pick letters, click to copy them, and paste to insert them; (b) insert or draw pictures to label and define at ever-increasing levels; (c) write a poem, story, rebus story, or book, and illustrate it. As their skills progress, in the middle and upper elementary grades, students can use Kid Pix to report research findings and illustrate creative writings by using the multimedia features.

Graphic Organizers for Grades 3–Adult

INSPIRATION® (http://www.inspiration.com/beta.html) is a visual learning tool that allows integrated diagramming and outlining views that work together to help students "quickly prioritize and rearrange ideas, helping them create clear, concise essays, reports and more." Inspiration is used for brainstorming, planning, organizing, outlining, prewriting, diagramming, concept mapping, and webbing.

Graphic Organizers for PreK–3

KidspirationTM (http://www.inspiration.com/kidspiration/index2.html) is a visual learning tool especially designed for emerging readers and writers. It helps students brainstorm, organize information, understand concepts and connections, create stories, and express and share their thoughts through webs, writing, and visuals. A picture view allows students to use an extensive library of pictures. The writing view allows students to write and integrate pictures. Students can use the audio tools to record and listen to their stories.

English/Language Lessons

▶ *Choose Your Own Story*[1]
English/Language Arts
Intermediate Tech Level for Grades 4–12

Lesson Summary: Several novels for children and adolescents today allow for choice within the story, creating multiple stories within one book. After enjoying a class book of this type, or after a short story unit (**ELA 3**), provide students with the opportunity to write collaboratively (**ELA 11**) on their stories (**ELA 4, 5**), reinforcing the ideas of plot and resolution.

ISTE NETS for Students— Standard 3: Technology Productivity Tools. Students use productivity tools to collaborate in constructing technology-enhanced models, preparing publications, and producing other creative works. **Standard 4: Technology Communications Tools.** Students use a variety of media and formats to communicate information and ideas effectively to multiple audiences.

Instructions

Use a story prompt to write the first few paragraphs (or sentences depending on the age group) of the story as a class. Model brainstorming, organization, and working in a group to develop the story. Set the scene and the tone for the story together. End this section of the story with the character(s) needing to make a decision between two possible choices. Type your story into PowerPoint or other hypermedia program (HyperStudio, or a series of Web pages). Illustrate with original scanned art, computer-generated drawings, or clip art

Break the class into two groups. Each group is assigned one alternative from the first part of the story and continues the story with that choice, concluding by leaving the character with two possible choices to continue. Each group types and illustrates their part of the story using the same software. Each of the two groups divides again into two groups. These new groups continue writing, again leaving the character with two possible choices, typing and illustrating their parts. Continue to break the class up into smaller groups until each individual student writes a possible ending for the story. After all of the possible endings are written, hyperlink the story together to create an interactive story with multiple endings.

Lower Tech Level: Type sections of story in Word. Insert bookmarks (under the Insert menu) to connect alternatives to the story that allow the reader to jump to the desired sections. Insert clip art to illustrate.

Higher Tech Level: Use Flash, LiveMotion, or Director to create the interactive story. Add animation, sound, and music. Publish to the Web or burn to a CD-ROM.

Teacher Education Connection: For Your Digital Portfolio: In your electronic portfolio, link strands of work that support your philosophy statement.

Kids in the News[2]
English/Language Arts
Intermediate Tech Level for Grades 5–8

Lesson Summary: Students use the library, online sources, and interviews (**ELA 8**) to research and write news stories and commercials as components of a school news program (**ELA 3**). To give students motivational opportunities for reading, writing, speaking, and listening, videotape this type of news program and present it to the school once a month.

ISTE NETS for Students—Standard 4: Technology Communications Tools. Students use telecommunications to collaborate, publish, and interact with peers, experts, and other audiences. **Standard 5: Technology Research Tools.** Students use technology to locate, evaluate, and collect information from a variety of sources. Copyright © 2000, ISTE. All rights reserved.

Instructions

- Research: Discuss some possible news reports and commercials related to school activities that advertise school events or fund-raisers. Make a list of suggestions and ask for volunteers to research, write, and report on the topics. After the "news teams" prepare questions for their interviews, the teacher and class review and revise them. Students begin their research, interviewing school staff and students to obtain their information.

- Writing: After the information has been gathered, students work in groups to write their scripts, revising and editing until the final video is done. The teacher reviews the final scripts for accuracy and grammatical structure.

- Rehearsing and Taping: The teams decide who will present their stories and commercials and how they will be presented. A deadline is established for the final taping which must be met. The class as a whole decides the order for the newscast, and two students are selected to "anchor" the program. Students who will not be presenting the newscast have other assignments such as announcing, operating the camera, and directing. Finally, the whole crew rehearses together and the videotape is completed.

- Presenting the News: After taping is completed, the class develops a list of printed questions that other students may answer as they watch the show. The newscast is scheduled and shown to other classes. The presenters critique their own products, deciding what could be improved next time.

Lower Tech Level: Use Word to create a written newspaper.
Higher Tech Level: Insert digitized video clips to further illustrate a point.
Teacher Education Connection: For Your Digital Portfolio: Interview people of different generations about their schooling. Use digitized segments to compare their information with history of education coursework.

---

[2] Adapted from "Kid-to-Kid News: A Video Language Arts Project" by D. Bullock, from *The Computing Teacher*, (now *Learning & Leading with Technology)* Vol. 20, no. 6, pp. 27–28, 55, copyright © 1996, ISTE (International Society for Technology in Education), 800.336.5191 (US & Canada) or 541.302.3777 (Int'l), iste@iste.org, www.iste.org. All rights reserved. Permission does not constitute an endorsement by ISTE.

Critics Corner Via E-Mail[3]
English/Language Arts
Beginning Tech Level for Grades 9–12

Lesson Summary: Improve critical thinking and writing skills by evaluating a piece of literature (**ELA 5**). This unique strategy may capture the interest of unmotivated readers. An examination of online critiques (**ELA 8**) and collaboration with other students on literary critiques via e-mail provide that extra interest. Connecting the subject matter to topics connected with special events (e. g., mystery stories or Gothic tales during October; love and romance during February; sports during various playoff seasons) also provokes interest.

ISTE NETS for Students— Standard 3: Technology Productivity Tools. Students use productivity tools to collaborate in constructing technology-enhanced models, prepare publications, and produce other creative works. Copyright © 2000, ISTE. All rights reserved.

Instructions
- Preparation: Set up a mail distribution list of students in your school or student e-pals elsewhere, who will receive the critiques, making sure that all students will send and receive a critique. Students can locate online critiques or reviews of stories, books, or movies to understand the critical review process. (**Check the school's Internet safe-use policies** before establishing e-pals.)
- Assignment: Each student is assigned a different short story written at the student's independent reading level and completes a 1–2 paragraph critique of the story to be shared with others via e-mail. Encourage them to write about what they think of the story, e.g., how well they feel it was written and what emotions and thoughts it elicited from them.
- Evaluation: When drafts are complete, have students exchange critiques with another student by e-mail, look for standard writing elements and those associated with reviews or critiques, provide feedback, and return the critique to the writer. When students receive theirs, they make revisions and the teacher uses a printout to check students' work. Save it for the students' portfolios. Students can then create a book or movie review.

Lower Tech Level: Students read hard copy of a story, book, movie review, and/or exchange hard copies of papers for a blind review.
Higher Tech Level: To edit, students use editing tools of word-processing documents. Finished critiques are cataloged and posted on the class Web site.

Teacher Education Connection: For Your Digital Portfolio: Use the process above to critique an online article on educational reform.

---

[3] **Adapted from:** Daniels, J., and Bryan, J. (1992). Critics corner. *The Florida Technology in Education Quarterly, 4*(2), 59–60.

Animated Poetry[4]
English/Language Arts
Intermediate Tech Level for Grades 4–12

Lesson Summary: As a culminating activity for a unit of study on poetry, students write or select an expressive poem **(ELA 4)** and use the appropriate technology to animate it to extend meaning **(ELA 8)**.

ISTE NETS for Students— Standard 3: Technology Productivity Tools. Students use technology tools to enhance learning, increase productivity, and promote creativity. Copyright © 2000, ISTE. All rights reserved.

Instructions

- Write a poem at least 4 lines in length, but not necessarily rhyming. The poem could be Cinquain, Haiku, limerick, concrete, or free poetry in form.
- Create individual slides for each poem. Use Windows Paint, KidPix, PhotoShop, or another graphics program to begin your animated poem.
- Create an image that includes the first line of your poem (or your title if you have one), and the illustrations you have chosen for that line. Images may be clip art, original art, found art digitally scanned, or art drawn on the computer using software graphics tools.
- Create a new folder named "poem" and save the file as "a001".
- Make a second slide by using the first slide and saving it as "a002". Write the second line of your poem, adjust or change the illustrations, and save.
- Continue making new slides from the previous slide and changing the name of the file. Add a new line of your poem for each slide. When you reach "a009", name the next file "a010".
- Using an animation program, assemble the still slides into one file that shows each slide for a set period of time. This will create the illusion of movement! (See http://www.crayonsoft.com/ for a free demo of MagicViewer Animation Software.)

Lower Tech Level: Illustrate poetry without animation. Type original or published poem into Word, KidPix, or other software. Illustrate using clip art, scanned images, or graphics tools.

Higher Tech Level: Use Flash, LiveMotion, or HotMedia to create an animation including sounds and music.

Teacher Education Connection: For Your Digital Portfolio: Animate a philosophy or classroom behavior management plan for your digital portfolio.

---

[4] **Sources:** Lori Schock, Computer Studies Instructor, Hadley Middle School, Wichita, KS. http://hadley.usd259.org/schock/vday.html; and Beth Adamson, 4/5 Classroom Teacher, Mueller Elementary School, Wichita, KS. http://www.crosswinds.net/~muellerelem/adamson/cinquian/cin.html

Writing through Webbing[5]
English/Language Arts
Intermediate Tech Level for Grades K–5

Lesson Summary: This lesson addresses the problem very young students have with beginning writing. They have a lot to say, but it is often difficult for them to get started. Through the following procedures, teachers introduce their students to a five-step process and encourage them to use it in writing **(ELA 5)**. The five steps include (1) Think, (2) Draw, (3) Tell, (4) Write, and (5) Share.

ISTE NETS for Students— Standard 3: Technology Productivity Tools. Students use technology tools to enhance learning, increase productivity, and promote creativity. Copyright © 2000, ISTE. All rights reserved.

Instructions

- Preparation to Write: At the beginning of the school year when students are excited about meeting new people, take a photo of each student in the class with a digital camera, or scan a regular photo in order to insert the pictures in written documents. Model how to use Inspiration or Kidspiration to create a graphic organizer Web of information about each student. Encourage students to think about specific content, describing themselves to others in terms of their favorite food, sports, TV shows, pets, vacations, future plans, etc.

- Planning through Webbing: Place each student's digital picture in the center of the student's graphic organizer Web and print each one. As students **Think** about what to tell about themselves, the printed chart serves to graphically organize the student's ideas **(Draw)**. Students then branch out from their picture with their ideas using Inspiration's rapid-fire method **(Tell)**. If students don't type, they can record their voices as they speak about their ideas in Kidspiration.

- Writing Activities: Using the information in the web, students begin a summary about themselves **(Write)**. They choose the font, size, and color of type for their document. The teacher/paraprofessional of upper-grade students enters the information into a word processing file as the students dictate it. Students work with the teacher or assistant to correct spelling and prepare a final copy to print out and present **(Share)** to the whole class.

Lower Tech Level: After the student's picture is placed in the center of the graphic organizing web, have the student draw his/her identifiers on the paper.
Higher Tech Level: Encourage students to create an entire Web in Kidspiration.
Teacher Education Connection: For Your Digital Portfolio: Create an Inspiration or Kidspiration Web to introduce yourself to your teacher education class, or to your own students in student teaching or teaching.

---

[5] **Adapted from** "A Powerful Web to Weave--Developing Writing Skills for Elementary Students" by C. Etchinson, from *Learning & Leading with Technology,* Vol. 23, no.3, pp. 14–15, copyright © 1996, ISTE (International Society for Technology in Education), 800.336.5191 (US & Canada) or 541.302.3777 (Int'l), iste@iste.org, www.iste.org. All rights reserved. Permission does not constitute an endorsement by ISTE.

Language and Technology Skills Check
English/Language Arts
Beginning Tech Level – Any Grade

Lesson Summary: During the opening routine of a class, many teachers ask students to complete reflective journals or a *Daily Oral Language (DOL)* activity (ELA 4, 5, 6). This is an opportune time to work on keyboarding skills. If you have only one computer, rotate the students through in an organized way. If you have several computers in your classroom, use this assignment as a learning center and rotate groups through the computer station allowing a week or two for each group. If you have access to a mobile lab or a computer lab, consider using this lesson as an introduction to keyboarding and word processing.

ISTE NETS for Students— Standard 1: Basic Operations and Concepts. Students demonstrate a sound understanding of the nature and operation of technology systems. Students are proficient in the use of technology. Copyright © 2000, ISTE. All rights reserved.

Instructions
- Determine your students' present skill levels in grammar and word processing skills (typing, formatting, using headers or footers, adding tables, adding graphics, etc.).
- Create a Word document of sentences or paragraphs on a topic relevant to your area of study. (Students can also be asked to type their spelling words, definitions, and create sentences using the words. Add a couple of writing prompts for extra credit for those students who work faster.)
- Place errors in the sentences or paragraphs appropriate for the level of your students. Print out a copy of your paragraph.
- Have the students retype the document, editing as they type.
- Students will be evaluated on their language skills and their keyboarding skills.

Lower Tech Level: Type the assignment.

Higher Tech Level: Include instructions for formatting the text when editing is completed. For example: (1) name— Arial, 12pt— is right justified. (2) date on the following line, same formatting. (3) title— Arial, 16 pt— bold, centered. (4) Document— Arial, 10pt— is left justified. Additional instructions might include headers, footers, tables, graphics, and wrapping text around graphics.

Teacher Education Connection: For Your Digital Portfolio: Document your keyboarding skills and experiences with different pieces of software.

Integrated English/Language Arts Lessons

▶ *The Real Story*
An Integrated English/Language Arts Unit on Human Issues
Intermediate Tech Level for Grades 5–8

Lesson Summary: Read a chapter novel to students involving human issues (death, poverty, prejudice, age) **(ELA 1; NCSS 1, 3)**. Build a model **(ELA 3, 5)**.

ISTE NETS for Students— Standard 3: Technology Productivity Tools. Students use technology tools to enhance learning, increase productivity, and promote creativity. Students use productivity tools to collaborate in constructing technology-enhanced models, prepare publications, and produce other creative works. Copyright © 2000, ISTE. All rights reserved.

Instructions

- Read a novel to the children over the period of 2–3 weeks, discussing the human issues involved in the story. Several examples are provided below.
- Choose key scenes that convey the meaningful information from the book.
- Break the class into groups, assigning each group one of the scenes.
- The first task of the group is to briefly explain in writing what happens in their assigned scene. (Younger students may need older students or adult volunteers to help with this writing.)
- Once this part of the story is written, students determine what scene or scenes are needed to tell their story and prepare backdrops, props, to fit the scenes. Students create a storyboard (set of scenes or pictures that tell their portion of the story).
- Students create clay characters to display the issues and place them into the scenes. A picture is taken of each scene, making only small changes in the scene from picture to picture. (Set scene, shoot, reset, shoot.)
- From the initial writing, their recall of the story, and the characters, students complete the narration.

Lower Tech Level: Use puppets and a puppet stage to tell and retell the story. Videotape the play to show to other classes.
Higher Tech Level: Add digitized sound effects or background music to the show.
Teacher Education Connection: For Your Digital Portfolio: In a children's literature class, include clay animation as a method of storytelling.

Human Issue Novels

Houston, Jeanne Wakatsuki, & Houston, J. D. *Farewell to Manzinar*
Park, B. *Mick Harte Was Here*
Taylor, M. *Roll of Thunder Hear My Cry*
Voight, C. *Homecoming, Dicey's Song, Solitary Blue*
Yates, E. *Amos Fortune, Free Man*

Periodicals for Kids – Current Events
An Integrated English/Language Arts Lesson
Beginning Tech Level for All Grades

Lesson Summary: Use online periodicals for students to stimulate current events discussions in class (**ELA 1; NCSS 3**). These can be viewed individually at computers during a rotation of centers, as a whole class in a computer lab, as a whole class in the classroom using a projection device or electronic whiteboard, or downloaded onto PDAs using AvantGo software. Students share what they find with others using some form of media.

ISTE NETS for Students— Standard 5: Technology Research Tools. Students use technology to locate, evaluate, and collect information from a variety of sources. Students use technology tools to process data and report results. **Standard 4: Technology Communications Tools.** Students use a variety of media and formats to communicate information and ideas effectively to multiple audiences. Copyright © 2000, ISTE. All rights reserved.

Instructions

- Preview online periodicals. Determine those with appropriate content for the age of your students.
- **Check the school's Internet safe-use policies.**
- Make a list of guiding questions that will serve the students on their news exploration. Let students choose the question they want to explore or place them in small learning groups to select a question.
- Allow time for students to research answers to their questions, compile the information, document sources appropriately, and report their results.
- Provide the students with multiple technology resources from which to choose to show the answers to their questions. The simplest is a written report, the more complicated a video or slide news show.
- Provide time in class to present the findings. Invite other classes in when appropriate.

Weekly Reader	http://www.weeklyreader.com/
Scholastic News Online	http://www.scholastic.com/scholasticnews/
Time For Kids	http://www.timeforkids.com/
Sports Illustrated For Kids	http://www.sikids.com/index.html

Lower Tech Level: Present the findings in a written report with an oral presentation. Publish written reports as a class magazine.
Higher Tech Level: Present the findings in a taped newscast.
Teacher Education Connection: For Your Digital Portfolio: Locate online periodicals appropriate for your content area. Create and maintain a database in which to include information about the sources and the articles.

▶ Photo Field Trip
An Integrated English/Language Arts Lesson
Beginning Tech Level for Grades K–3

Lesson Summary: As a culminating experience after an in-depth study of a topic, many schools plan field trips (**ELA 3**) to the farm, the zoo, the science museum, or the pumpkin patch for the younger students. Before the trip, generate a list of questions that the students want answered or things they think they will see (**ELA 7; NCTM; NAS NCR 3**). Consider rotating the years for the field trips and saving questions, pictures, and answers for digital virtual field trips for the students who don't actually go to the places or as story starters for students before, during, or after study of a topic.

ISTE NETS for Students— Standard 5: Technology Research Tools. Students use technology to locate, evaluate, and collect information from a variety of sources. Students use technology tools to process data and report results. Copyright © 2000, ISTE. All rights reserved.

Instructions
- Select a site for the field trip. Work with students to generate a list of questions they have and a list of things they think they will see. Encourage students to think about sounds and smells as well as sights: colors, shapes and sizes.
- Type the questions and save as a word processed document. Take copies of the questions along on the trip to serve as guidelines for conversation, examination, and exploration.
- Take digital photographs or short video clips of the sights students find as answers to their questions.
- Download the pictures, save to disk, and post them as answers to their own questions.
- Save the digital pictures in a digital scrapbook or the photographs in a photo album for next year's students.

Lower Tech Level: Print questions on 4" x 5" index cards. Take photographs of the sights. Match the questions to the photographic answer, or use the photographs as story starters to answer the questions posed before the trip.

Higher Tech Level: Make a virtual field trip. Post the questions, the pictures, sound clips, video clips, and the written responses to the questions on a class Web site.

Teacher Education Connection: For Your Digital Portfolio: Document each of your field experiences with photographs (the school, the artifacts, and the students), mission statements, and demographic information. To include student photographs, get permission from the school and/or parents.

For an example see a virtual field trip to the fire station:
> http://education.wichita.edu/twitherspo/firestation_vft/index.htm

▶ Using the Internet to Guide the Writing Process
An Integrated English/Language Arts Lesson
Beginning Tech Level for Grades 7–12

Lesson Summary: Following the study of the Civil War, students are asked to write a paper using a topic selected from the University of Virginia Center for Digital History's Valley of the Shadow project which provides research questions and primary source documents to search for answers. Students also use the Internet for help in webbing and constructing the paper.

ISTE NETS for Students— Standard 3: Technology Productivity Tools. Students use technology tools to enhance learning, increase productivity, and promote creativity. Students use productivity tools to collaborate in constructing technology-enhanced models, prepare publications, and produce other creative works. **Standard 5: Technology Research Tools.** Students use technology to locate, evaluate, and collect information from a variety of sources. Students use technology tools to process data and report results. Copyright © 2000, ISTE. All rights reserved.

Instructions
- **Check the school's Internet safe-use policies.**
- Read through the Valley of the Shadow information available online at http://jefferson.village.virginia.edu/vshadow2/
- Write a set of simple instructions for this project in a Word document. Link the sights so that when the students are at a computer with Internet accessibility and click on the sites, they are sent there directly. Those written directions should include
    - The purpose of the assignment— to investigate and report first hand information about the Civil War.
    - Select a guiding question.
    http://jefferson.village.virginia.edu/vcdh/teaching/vclassroom/vclasscontents.html
    - Select a graphic organizer.
    http://www.ncrel.org/sdrs/areas/issues/students/learning/lr1grorg.htm
    http://www.teachervision.com/lesson-plans/lesson-6293.html
    - Guidelines for writing a paper
    http://www.geocities.com/SoHo/Atrium/1437/index.html
    - The format and requirements for the paper in the form of a rubric.

Lower Tech Level: Select topics from the UVA site, but locate information in text, library, and encyclopedias. (It would be interesting to do this first and then compare the information to that in the primary source documents.)

Higher Tech Level: Design a newsletter that uses the questions as headlines and the papers as responses. Insert primary source photos when available.

Teacher Education Connection: For Your Digital Portfolio: Research the history of the role of teaching through primary source documents located at UVA or elsewhere.

INTEGRATING ISTE STANDARDS INTO MATHEMATICS

The **National Council of Teachers of Math (NCTM)** is an organization whose mission is to provide the vision and leadership necessary to ensure a mathematics education of the highest quality for all students. *Principles and Standards for School Mathematics* (2000) provides its "guidelines for excellence in mathematics education and issues a call for all students to engage in more challenging mathematics. Its content is extended online through the E-Standards (standards.nctm.org) and Illuminations (illuminations.nctm.org)."

The math standards are used in accreditation processes in many states and are approved by the National Council for the Accreditation of Teacher Education (NCATE) that provides a voluntary accreditation for over 2,000 colleges of education in the US (http://www.ncate.org/).

Recognizing that everyday life is increasingly mathematical and technological, in their vision for school mathematics, NCTM states that "Technology is an essential component of the environment." They visualize an environment where "Alone or in groups and with access to technology, they [students] work productively and reflectively, with the skilled guidance of their teachers to communicate their ideas and results effectively." Classrooms must have ready access to technology, "technologically-equipped for the twenty-first century" (http://standards.nctm.org/document/chapter1/index.htm). The theme of one of the six principles for school mathematics is technology, recognizing that it "is essential in teaching and learning mathematics; it influences the mathematics that is taught, and enhances students' learning." (http://standards.nctm.org/document/chapter2/index.htm)

NCTM suggests that PreK–2 students should begin work with calculators and that computers help provide feedback and connections between representations. In addition, they note that computers are "especially helpful for learners with physical limitations or those who interact more comfortably with technology than with classmates." (http://standards.nctm.org/document/chapter4/index.htm)

By grades 9–11, NCTM notes that students should use spreadsheets, data-gathering devices, computer algebra systems, and graphing utilities as well as accessing online mathematical information related to the "federal budget, school-board budgets, mutual-fund values, and local used-car prices." Advanced high school math is preparation for advanced math courses and careers in graphic design, architecture, carpentry, systems scheduling, financial planning, pharmaceuticals, and for economists, marketing experts, and political advisers. (http://standards.nctm.org/document/chapter7/index.htm)

All **ISTE NETS for Student Standards** readily align with the NCTM mathematics standards.

Technology Tools for Mathematics

Spreadsheets for Children and Adults

Spreadsheets often come as part of a package or suite of programs (**Microsoft Office or Corel WordPerfect Suite**),and are convenient tools for teachers and students. For purposes of mathematics, spreadsheets can be used for timelines, graphing, calculating using formulas, probability, exploring problems, geometric transformations, functions, probability, and statistics. **FreshPond Education, Inc.** provides teachers with ways to include spreadsheets in instruction. http://www.freshpond.net/treasures/math/spreadsheet/default.htm

Graph Club

(http://www.tomsnyder.com/products/productdetail.asp?PS=GRPGRT) Allows younger students to create five different kinds of graphs: table, picture, bar, line, and circle to represent findings, compare findings with others, hypothesize future findings, etc.

Graph Master

(http://www.tomsnyder.com/products/productdetail.asp?PS=GRAMAS) allows students to use nine different graph types; explore mean, median, mode, and range; solve problems and make decisions using graphs; and write conclusions.

Tessellation Exploration

http://www.tomsnyder.com/products/productdetail.asp?PS=TESEXP Geometry concepts are reinforced as students create two-dimensional Tessellations and watch them slide, turn, flip, and glide on the screen. Students also explore tessellations that exist in the world, such as honeycombs, tile floors, and brick buildings.

TimeLiner 5.0

http://www.tomsnyder.com/products/productdetail.asp?PS=TIMV50 Timeliner makes it easy to create, illustrate, and print timelines. Enter events and dates, and it puts them in chronological order.

Geometer's Sketchpad

(http://www.keypress.com/sketchpad/) Geometer's Sketchpad allows students to construct figures ranging from simple diagrams to working models of the Pythagorean Theorem, perspective drawings, tessellations, fractals, animated sine waves, etc. It fits well with geometry, but also with algebra, trigonometry, calculus, art, and science.

Logo

(http://el.www.media.mit.edu/groups/logo-foundation/) Logo is a continually evolving family of programming languages that are founded on the constructivist educational philosophy. Several Logo-based programs allow students to create rich simulations and programs such as **MicroWorlds** (http://microworlds.com/) and **Terrapin Logo** (http://terrapinlogo.com/)

Using Imaging Technology in the Math Classroom

Mathematics

Intermediate Tech Level, Grades 6–12

The Center for Image Processing in Education (CIPE) is a nonprofit organization dedicated to furthering the study of image processing in the classroom (http://www.cipe.com). They publish a series of instructional materials that use image technology. Each lesson includes complete lesson plans and the images needed for the plan. The lessons also require NIH Image (Macintosh) or Scion Image (Windows 95/98/NT) software, which are both public domain software.

NIH Image (Macintosh)
http://rsb.info.nih.gov/nih-image/

Scion Image (Windows 95/98/NT)
http://www.scioncorp.com/

Samples of free downloadable lessons from CIPE are shown here. For more information, visit their Web site (http://www.cipe.com).

Going in Circles

Lesson: http://evisual.org/Software/SoftIPLessons/Circles.pdf
Image Files: http://evisual.org/Software/SoftIPLessons/Circles.zip

In Going in Circles, from HIP® Mathematics, students discover the origin of pi by using NIH Image or Scion Image to measure the diameter and circumference of circular objects.

On Tour in America

Lesson: http://evisual.org/Software/SoftIPLessons/OnTour.pdf
Image Files: http://evisual.org/Software/SoftIPLessons/OnTour.zip

Students will learn about coordinate systems, measurement, and labeling techniques. This lesson, a sample from Discovering Image Processing, can be used in a mathematics class, or to teach measurement skills in science, technology or geography. Students play the role of band members planning their band's first national tour. After using coordinates to locate and label major cities, students measure distance and estimate the time schedule of the trip.

Mathematics Lessons

▶ *A Chess Club by E-Mail*[6]
Mathematics
Beginning Tech Level for Grades 5–12

Lesson Summary: Practice problem-solving strategies and skills by playing chess via e-mail. (Check the school online policies to make sure students have permission to be on e-mail.) Chess notation, a system of notation long employed to play through the mail or on the phone, is a good activity to teach along with mathematical ordered pairs **(NCTM)**. Computers allow instant play via e-mail. Standard time is one move per day per game for e-mail games, taking a long time, but allowing for much conversation and strategy planning.

ISTE NET for Students— Standard 4: Technology Communications Tools. Students use telecommunications to collaborate, publish, and interact with peers, experts, and other audiences. Copyright © 2000, ISTE. All rights reserved.

Instructions

- Students need to know how to play chess and have knowledge of how to write the chess moves (chess notation). The teachers involved may find it helpful to create a brief player's manual that describes how to write the moves and tells the rules of playing chess by computer.
- To allow more students to be involved, divide each class into four teams, allowing members to consult on each move.
- Chess is not a fast activity, so games take more than one session. Ten moves per hour is a common rate of play when using "chat" mode. When responding to an e-mail move, teams may need 15–20 minutes or longer to strategize before making a move. At one move per day, it could take from one to three months to complete a game. Use the following procedures:
  - Write, publish, and field-test the player's manual.
  - Contact schools to join the E-mail Chess Club. Each class studies the manual. The teachers arrange a time to play "friendly match."
  - Each class is then split into four teams with the roles of player, recorder, and observers in each group. Chessboards are set up near the computer, connected to e-mail for easy transmission of moves.
  - Have experts help monitor and assist with games and transmissions.
  - Establish the e-mail connection.
  - Decide who will play the white and black pieces in all games.
  - Rounds proceed orderly with all moves for each school sent before receiving school responds with their moves.
  - Consider setting up tournaments, leagues, weekend play, or newsletters.

Lower Tech Level: Use e-mail only, one move a day.

Higher Tech Level: Use live chats or webcams to facilitate the plan.

Teacher Education Connection: For Your Digital Portfolio: Work with cooperating teachers by e-mail planning for and reflecting on your teaching.

---

[6] **Adapted from:** Gittelson, H. (1993). The FIRN chess club. *The Florida Technology in Education Quarterly, 5*(3), 64–66.

What's the Cost?
Mathematics
Beginning Tech Level for Grades 4–8

Lesson Summary: While studying various states and/or events in the United States, students plan a trip to an event (located in online newspapers) or a place (located on online maps). Students determine the mileage for two routes (scenic and direct) **(NCTM)**, the miles per gallon of gasoline required for two different cars, and the amount of time it will take to get there, driving at 60 miles per hour, to determine the longest and shortest trips **(NCTM)**. Information is presented in a summary paragraph and an accompanying table **(NCTM)**.

ISTE NETS for Students— Standard 2: Social, Ethical, and Human Issues. Students develop positive attitudes toward technology uses that support lifelong learning, collaboration, personal pursuits, and productivity. **Standard 4: Technology Communications Tools.** Students use a variety of media and formats to communicate information and ideas effectively to multiple audiences. **Standard 5: Technology Research Tools.** Students use technology to locate, evaluate, and collect information from a variety of sources. Students use technology tools to process data and report results. **Standard 6: Technology Problem-solving and Decision-making Tools.** Students use technology resources for solving problems and making informed decisions. Copyright © 2000, ISTE. All rights reserved.

Instructions
- **Check the school's Internet safe-use policies.**
- While connected to a current events, geography, or other social studies lesson, have students use online sources to select an event or place to visit.
- Locate MapQuest to determine a scenic and a direct route. http://www.mapquest.com
- For both routes, calculate the number of miles to the event or place.
- Select two different cars.
- Visit automobile sites to determine the gas mileage for two different cars.
- Locate information about gas prices along the way.
- Calculate the estimated amount and cost of gasoline needed.
- Calculate the amount of time it will take at 60 miles per hour for both cars.
- Place all information in a table.
- Summarize the information in a paragraph to display with the table.

Lower Tech Level: Use newspapers and paper maps to locate event and mileage.
Higher Tech Level: Set the functions in a spreadsheet to calculate the equations. Prepare a travel brochure to advertise each trip or event.
Teacher Education Connection: For Your Digital Portfolio: Locate the time, location, and purpose of the annual conference for the national organization in your content area. Draft a grant proposal to attend, using a table to show the expenses and a summary paragraph to explain the purpose.

Mathematics
Beginning Tech Level for Grades K–5

Lesson Summary: Students use Kid Pix to illustrate and solve simple number problems **(NCTM)**.

ISTE NETS for Students— Standard 6: Technology Problem-solving and Decision-making Tools. Students use technology resources for solving problems and making informed decisions. Copyright © 2000, ISTE. All rights reserved.

Instructions
- Demonstrate the use of the stamping tools in KidPix, focusing on the number stamps and the rubber stamps.

Addition Problems
- First, students use the number stamps to stamp out the simple addition problem in a sentence format, leaving the solution empty.
- Second, students use the rubber stamps to stamp the corresponding number of objects next to each number.
- Third, students put the number answer in the proper place and stamp the number of objects next to the answer, noting the answer.
- Check to see that the same number of objects are on both sides of the equal (=) sign.
- Have the children change the numbers in the first part of the sentence around and see if the answer is different. Have the children change the addition symbol to a subtraction symbol. Erase the number of rubber stamp pictures for the answer and stamp the correct number.

Subtraction, Multiplication, and Simple Division Problems
- Challenge students to illustrate subtraction problems and verbally communicate their strategy to you.

Lower Tech Level: Write the math equations for the students and just have them stamp the correct number of objects.
Higher Tech Level: Instead of using the rubber stamps have children use Kid Pix to draw their own pictures using the drawing tools.
Teacher Education Connection: For Your Digital Portfolio: Use Kid Pix to create a set of flash cards, charts, or posters for use in your methods courses and student teaching.

Robotics
Mathematics
Intermediate to High Level for Grades 4–12

Lesson Summary: In this lesson students use the Lego Mindstorms Robotics Invention System to build a simple Pathfinder robot and program it first to two required moves and secondly to solve problems (**NCTM**).

ISTE NETS for Students— Standard 6, Technology Problem-solving and Decision-making Tools. Students use technology resources for solving problems and making informed decisions. Students employ technology in the development of strategies for solving problems in the real world. Copyright © 2000, ISTE. All rights reserved.

Instructions
- Provide each group of 3–4 students with a Lego Mindstorms Robotics Invention System.
- Require students to develop and complete an inventory of all the pieces. All pieces in the kit are then their responsibility throughout the project.
- Have students build a simple Pathfinder robot. Building instructions are included in the Constructopedia.
- Program the robot to go forward for two seconds and stop.
- Challenge students to make the Pathfinder spin. They would need to program one wheel to stop or reverse.
- Ask students to control the spin to make the Pathfinder turn a 90-degree turn. This will take some trial and error, changing the codes for the amount of power and time the robotic motor is stopped or reversed.
- When students have completed a program to make their robot go forward for two seconds and then complete a 90-degree turn to make an "L," ask them how they can take this procedure and program their robot to make a square. A square would be a repeat of this procedure four times. The robot will start and stop in the same position.
- Upon completion of the projects, have students dismantle the robots and catalog all pieces and sign the inventory sheet before returning them to the boxes.

Lower Level Project: Have students program the robot to stop and go, trying to predict and explain its cumulative distance.

Higher Level Extension: After programming the robot to complete a square, program the robot to complete a squared figure eight. This will take some thinking because the fourth repeat will no longer be a two second forward and then a turn but rather it will be four seconds long to begin the first line of the second square. Then, the rest of the commands will be flipped.

Lesson Summary: Trigonometry is a branch of mathematics in which students often are asked to do many activities they do not understand conceptually. This activity is designed to let students use the *Geometer's Sketchpad* software to gain a better conceptual grounding in some common trigonometry principles. Students use a "clinometer" to measure the height of various objects in and around the school **(NCTM)** and compare their results in preparation to see how high launched rockets go.

ISTE NETS for Students— Standard 6: Technology Problem-solving and Decision-making Tools. Students use technology resources for solving problems and making informed decisions. Students employ technology in the development of strategies for solving problems in the real world. Copyright © 2000, ISTE. All rights reserved.

Instructions
Measuring the Height of a Telephone Pole

- Demonstrate how to use a clinometer by measuring off a certain distance from a telephone pole and using the clinometer to measure the angle of elevation.
- Have students take a reading and draw a triangle to show the scale drawing of the pole indicating the angle of elevation (checks for accuracy and logic).
- After they do the drawing, students realize that the clinometer reading gave them angle ACB, not the angle of elevation, CAB, they needed.
- Ask them to look at a "dynamic triangle" created with the *Geometer's Sketchpad* software. In this drawing, the triangle is dynamic because dragging the vertex to various positions can change it.
- Let students experiment with this drawing to lead them to the insight: you get the angle of elevation by taking the clinometer reading and subtracting it from 90 degrees. This allows them to solve the problem with the pole.
- Create a digital image of the pole just measured. Import the digital file of the image into the *Geometer's Sketchpad* software. The students realize the snapshot is a smaller version of their real drawing and that the *Geometer's Sketchpad* software can help them measure it.
- Students use a "stretch factor" to multiply the figures in the smaller drawing to get the actual figures for the subsequent drawings.

Using a Digital Image to Measure Height
- Use a digital camera to take a digital image of the pole they just measured.

---

[7] **Adapted from** "Measuring Heights, or What Trigonometry Tables are All About" by I. Charischak, from *Learning & Leading with Technology*, Vol. 23, no. 5, pp. 13–16, copyright © 1996, ISTE (International Society for Technology in Education), 800.336.5191 (US & Canada) or 541.302.3777 (Int'l), iste@iste.org, www.iste.org. All rights reserved. Permission does not constitute an endorsement by ISTE.

- Import the file into the *Geometer's Sketchpad* software. The students realize the snapshot is a smaller version of their real drawing and that the software can help them measure it.
- Instruct the students that they should use a "stretch factor" to multiply the figures in the smaller drawing to get the actual figures for the subsequent drawings.
- Show them that they can do this with a tangent. Since a tangent is a line that touches a circle in one and only one place, the stretch factor can be obtained by getting the measurement of the side corresponding to the pole for any angle of elevation.
- Show them how they can draw a tangent and use a table of tangents stored in a spreadsheet file to obtain the stretch factor.
- Have students complete the following steps to do a dynamic drawing with the *Geometer's Sketchpad* software:
    - Draw a circle with the diameter of one unit.
    - Draw a radius AB.
    - Highlight line AB and point B.
    - Draw the perpendicular line, then hide the line.
    - Place a point C on the line.
    - Draw segments AC and BC and measure angle BAC and BC.

BC is the tangent of angle CAB. The radius BA equals 1, so the length of the baseline will be the stretch factor. Students can find any measure they need by dragging the vertex up or down until they have the desired angle. Then the length of BC (the missing side) is the length multiplied by the stretch factor. The students realize they can compare the measurements of this triangle with the values in the table of tangents and get a tangent length to correspond to the angle of elevation. When they multiply the tangent times the baseline length, they will have their answer.

Measuring the Height of Launched Rockets

- After students have constructed rockets, set aside a day to launch them, challenging students to take a digital photograph of their rocket at the peak of its launch. Or, use a digital video camera to take a movie of the launch so that you are able to snap a still from the video showing the rocket at its peak height.
- Follow the instructions above to measure the height of the rocket.

Required Resources:

Clinometer, *Geometer's Sketchpad* (Key Curriculum Press) software; digital camera or video camera; table of tangents on a spreadsheet

Integrated Mathematics Lessons

When Microworlds and Real Worlds Collide[8]

Integrated Lesson for Mathematics
Intermediate Tech Level for Grades K–4

Lesson Summary: Students use a Logo-based hypermedia software to develop a bridge-building proposal for their local community. They explore geometric shapes by identifying them in real-world structures (**NCTM**), conduct research on a topic (**ELA 7**), summarize and present findings in a multimedia format (**ELA 8**), and use data from real-world structures to develop multimedia simulations of bridge structures and operations (**NCTM**).

ISTE NETS for Students— Standard 4: Technology Communication Tools. Students use a variety of media and formats to communicate information and ideas effectively to multiple audiences. **Standard 5: Technology Research Tools.** Students use technology to locate, evaluate, and collect information from a variety of sources. Students use technology tools to process data and report results. Students evaluate and select new information resources and technological innovations based on the appropriateness for specific tasks. **Standard 6: Technology Problem-solving and Decision-making Tools.** Students employ technology in the development of strategies for solving problems in the real world. Copyright © 2000, ISTE. All rights reserved.

Instructions

Community Survey

- Students first survey community members about their attitudes toward a proposed new bridge and create spreadsheets to hold the survey and results.

Bridges in the Community

- Gather information about area bridges: historical documents, stories, poems.
- Study the shapes and designs of various bridges (connect to math class) and draw the bridges using drawing tools in a graphics program.
- Take a field trip to see the bridges being studied.

Designing Bridges

- Students design their own electronic bridge simulation using the *MicroWorlds Project Builder* (LCSI) software which includes the ability to manipulate the variables of angles, ratio, length, and speed to make objects move. Students construct bridges, add bridge traffic, and calculate estimates of the number of people who would cross the bridge in a given period.

Lower Tech Level: Construct models of bridges using building materials.
Higher Tech Level: Prepare a multimedia report to city commissioners.
Teacher Education Connection: For Your Digital Portfolio: Survey community members about local educational issues. Write local board members.

---

[8] **Adapted from:** "Does Cincinnati Need Another Bridge?" by D. Salisbury, from *Learning & Leading with Technology,* Vol. 23, no. 1, pp. 17–19, copyright © 1996, ISTE (International Society for Technology in Education), 800.336.5191 (US & Canada) or 541.302.3777 (Int'l), iste@iste.org, www.iste.org. All rights reserved. Permission does not constitute an endorsement by ISTE.

Shapes in the World
An Integrated Lesson for Mathematics
Beginning Tech Level for Grades K–4

Lesson Summary: Students create shapes and go on hunts to find them in their environment. Use Kid Pix to draw one shape of various sizes and paint (fill) with different colors and patterns **(Art)**, recognizing that all sizes and colors of shape are still the same shape **(NCTM; NAS NRC 1)**. Go on shape hunts in the classrooms, the schoolyards, the community, or the zoo, carrying the shape to remind them of their hunt, taking digital pictures of their found shape **(NAS NRC 3)**. Their hunt might also include spheres, cylinders, and cones.

ISTE NETS for Students— Standard 2: Social, Ethical, and Human Issues. Students understand the ethical, cultural, and societal issues related to technology. **Standard 3: Technology Productivity Tools.** Students use productivity tools to collaborate in constructing technology-enhanced models, prepare publications, and produce other creative works. **Standard 4: Technology Communications Tools.** Students use a variety of media and formats to communicate information and ideas effectively to multiple audiences. **Standard 5: Technology Research Tools.** Students use technology to locate, evaluate, and collect information from a variety of sources. Students use technology tools to process data and report results. Copyright © 2000, ISTE. All rights reserved.

Instructions

- Ask students to draw and paint several circles using a graphics program such as Kid Pix, helping them realize that circles are circles, no matter what color. Print out at least one of the circles to cut out for the next task.
- Give a group of three (P–K) students a small sack. Go on a shape hunt to gather things that are circles. Or students can be placed in small groups with an adult and a digital camera to explore the building, school grounds, farm, or zoo to locate circles in those environments. If they take pictures of people, they must tell the person why they are taking pictures and ask permission.
- Attach the found objects (or pictures) down the left-hand side of a bulletin board, labeling the object and using "is a circle" as the sentence ending for each statement about the object. "An Oreo is a circle."
- Younger students can use Kid Pix to draw their found object and label each to make a circle book. Older students each make a slide for each object. To develop this slide, they: a) insert their digital pictures into Kid Pix, b) label the picture, c) state that it is or has parts that are circles, and d) write a simple definition of the object. All slides are put together for a slide show.
- Present the book or slide show to the class and invited guests.

Lower Tech Level: Use the rubber stamp tool to stamp circles.
Higher Tech Level: Videotape the process. Edit, digitize small clips, and add voice narration to form a class "movie."
Teacher Education Connection: For Your Digital Portfolio: Use the strategy to design a lesson plan in your methods course.

Which Movement Counts the Most?[9]
Pedometers in Physical Education
An Integrated Math Lesson Easily Adapted for Any Grade Level

Lesson Summary: Each student will wear a pedometer/step counter during physical education class. At the end of each class, the students will use a personal data sheet to record the number of steps from their pedometer and describe their physical activity for the class period (**NASPE 3**). After 10 physical education classes, the students will "analyze" their data (**NCTM**). Using simple graphing methods, the students determine which activity will result in the greatest number of steps (**NASPE 4**). Older students may also determine how many minutes are needed to participate in each activity in order to reach 10,000 steps in one day (**NASPE 4; NCTM**).

ISTE NETS for Students— Standard 5: **Technology Research Tools.** Students use technology to locate, evaluate, and collect information from a variety of sources. Students use technology tools to process data and report results. **Standard 6. Technology Problem-solving and Decision-making Tools.** Students use technology resources for solving problems and making informed decisions. Copyright © 2000, ISTE. All rights reserved.

Instructions

- Wear a pedometer/step counter while teaching physical education or through the day as you teach any subject.
- Provide a pedometer/step counter for each student to wear during physical education class.
- At the end of the class, have students use a personal data sheet to record the number of steps from their pedometer, and then they can describe their physical activity for the class period.
- After 10 physical education classes, have students combine the data.
- Ask students to insert the data into a graphing program, using the activity as one axis and the number of steps as the other.
- Analyze the data and make recommendations from the results.
- Older students may determine the various configurations that allow reaching 10,000 steps in one day. (The latest research information indicates that 10,000 steps a day meets the guidelines set by the American College of Sports Medicine and the Centers for Disease Control and Prevention for physical activity.)

Lower Tech Level: Students can calculate and graph the information by hand.
Higher Tech Level: Students can record information onto spreadsheets loaded onto PDAs.
Teacher Education Connection: For Your Digital Portfolio: Locate content area standards to load into grading programs or onto PDAs.

---

[9] **Source:** Dr. Colleen Evans-Fletcher and Dr. Vicki Worrell, Department of Kinesiology and Sport Studies, Wichita State University, Wichita, Kansas.

INTEGRATING ISTE STANDARDS INTO SCIENCE

The **National Academy of Sciences: National Research Council (NAS NRC)** provides a set of science content standards for all students. Their vision is to have a scientifically literate populace. The main focus of the standards is on what students need to know, but they also focus on what teachers need to do and what the environment should be like. There is no doubt that students need to learn science to survive in our world (http://books.nap.edu/html/nses/html/overview.html).

The eight categories of content standards are (1) Unifying Concepts and Processes in Science; (2) Science as Inquiry; (3) Physical Science; (4) Life Science; (5) Earth and Space Science; (6) Science and Technology, (7) Science in Personal and Social Perspectives; (8) History and Nature of Science.

Specific references to technology occur in Standard 6 (Science and Technology) and Standard 7 (Science in Personal and Social Perspectives).

At an appropriate level, and as a result of activities, students in grades K–12 should develop abilities of technological design and understandings about science and technology. At an appropriate level and as a result of activities, K–4 students should develop an understanding of science and technology in local challenges, Grade 5–8 students should develop an understanding of science and technology in society, and Grade 9–12 students should develop an understanding of science and technology in local, national, and global challenges.

The **ISTE NETS for Student Standards** that most align with the NAS NRC Science Standards include **Standard 3, Technology Productivity Tools, Standard 4, Technology Communications Tools** for reporting and communicating results, **Standard 5, Technology Research Tools** for research; and **Standard 6, Technology Problem-solving and Decision-making Tools** for analysis.

Technology Tools for Science

Probeware

Students now have access to real-world data collection tools that are easy to use, compact, portable, and affordable. With probeware, students can unleash their creativity and enthusiasm and be problem solvers. Computer- and calculator-based interfaces with sensors can gather data by measuring light, heat, temperature, motion, pH, pressure, and much more. Data collection can occur instantaneously, overnight, or over a period of weeks or months. Because of probeware's portability, students can gather data in many situations and environments, which leads to more real-world meaningful experiences.

Spreadsheets for Children and Adults

Spreadsheets often come as part of a package or suite of programs (Microsoft Office or Corel WordPerfect Suite), and are convenient tools for teachers and students. Spreadsheets in the science classroom can be used to record and tabulate scientific data and graph the results.

Databases

Databases are useful in collecting similar data and information so that it can be sorted and related to other similar information. Databases can be used in the science classroom to keep track of equipment and materials, record experimental data, and relate information together.

Still Cameras

Digital images can be a powerful way to document information and scientific discovery. Students can use these images to communicate and share their learning. Digital images can be inserted into word processing documents, posted to the Web, sent by e-mail, added to multimedia presentations, or printed.

Digital Video Cameras

Digital video cameras allow students to record a process or event in its entirety and then play and watch the event again. This documentation can be edited to show the key events over time and compare to other documented discoveries.

Webcams

Webcams, or digital cameras that can be hooked up directly to your computer and feed live images to the screen, can be very helpful in the science classroom. Webcams are capable of recording digital video movies of classroom experiments that can be saved and viewed later for comparison or documentation. Webcams can also be set up to take a series of digital still images or digital video clips over time. This time-lapse photography can be used in many ways to enhance lessons and share information. Webcams can also be used for digital conferencing, allowing a classroom to interact with other classrooms over the Internet and share discoveries. Virtual guest lecturers can also be invited to use webcams to video conference with a group of students.

Using Imaging Technology in the Science Classroom
Intermediate Tech Level, Grades 6–12

The Center for Image Processing in Education (CIPE) is a nonprofit organization dedicated to furthering the study of image processing in the classroom (http://www.cipe.com). They publish a series of instructional materials that use image technology. Each set includes complete lesson plans and the images needed for the plan. The lessons also require NIH Image (Macintosh) or Scion Image (Windows 95/98/NT) software, which are both in the public domain.

NIH Image (Macintosh)
http://rsb.info.nih.gov/nih-image/

Scion Image (Windows 95/98/NT)
http://www.scioncorp.com/

Free downloadable lessons from CIPE are printed here. For further information, visit their Web site (http://www.cipe.com).

Earth Shots
Lesson: http://www.evisual.org/Instr/EnvSci/EarthShot.html

Students examine global satellite images and analyze urban sprawl, tropical rainforest deforestation, the disappearance and growth of inland seas, movements of glaciers, and other drastic environmental changes. Students discover firsthand the power of remote sensing for environmental monitoring and management.

ArcExplorer
Lesson: http://www.evisual.org/Instr/EnvSci/sheep/Bighorn.html

Students learn about bighorn sheep and their life cycle and habits. Then, they study highway traffic and the effects this has on bighorn sheep survival. Students analyze information and then propose solutions to the problem.

Use of Geographic Information Systems (GIS) technology, a computer-based tool employed by biologists and engineers, is integrated into the structure of this lesson. Students view photographs of bighorn sheep and real data collected by AZGF researchers and federal agencies and then use ArcExplorer, a public domain GIS data viewer, to analyze the data.

Animal Hands
Lesson: http://www.evisual.org/Software/SoftIPLessons/AnimalHands.pdf
Image Files: http://www.evisual.org/Software/SoftIPLessons/AnimalHands.zip

Animal Hands is an introductory lesson from HIP® Biology 1. Students use image processing to examine X-rays of hands, wings, hooves, and flippers to compare their structures and functions. Image processing allows them to change the way the information contained in the X-rays is displayed. They use a variety of techniques to study the detail in the images.

Brain's Blood Supply
Lesson: http://evisual.org/Software/SoftIPLessons/BrainBlood.pdf
Image Files: http://evisual.org/Software/SoftIPLessons/BrainBlood.zip

Brain's Blood Supply is a lesson from A&P Technologist. It introduces students to basic image enhancement tools such as false colorization, inversion of pixel values, and digital filters to sharpen, shadow, and find edges. In the second part of the lesson, students measure the diameter of the aorta and arteries in the neck, and then calculate the radius, cross-sectional area, and resistance for each vessel. After analyzing the data, they infer relationships between vessel size and relative blood flow.

Eruption Plumes of Io
Lesson: http://evisual.org/Software/SoftIPLessons/Erupt.pdf
Image Files: http://evisual.org/Software/SoftIPLessons/Erupt.zip

This lesson, from the sourcebook used at CIPE's image processing workshops, reinforces the idea that the laws of motion and gravitation are, indeed, universal. Io, one of Jupiter's moons, is famous for its active volcanoes. Students work with digital images radioed to Earth by the Voyager 1 and 2 spacecraft to enhance and measure Io's fountain-like plumes. Using their measurements, they determine the ejection velocity of the plume material. Students also look for changes in the plumes' activity over time.

Gel Electrophoresis
Lesson: http://evisual.org/Software/SoftIPLessons/Gel.pdf
Image Files: http://evisual.org/Software/SoftIPLessons/Gel.zip

Gel Electrophoresis is a lesson from Biotechnologist. In the lesson, students explore a series of images showing the techniques and concepts involved in separating molecules by size in an electric field. Then, the students analyze an actual movie of DNA molecules moving through an agarose gel.

Science Lessons

Animal Riddles[10]
Science
Beginning Tech Level for Grades K–5

Lesson Summary: Students are assigned an animal to research and present the information they find as a set of clues, which describe the animal's traits (**NAS NRC 4**). This set of clues is concluded with a statement, "Who am I?" A second sheet of paper has a picture drawn on it. Two slides are made: (1) the clues, and (2) a picture of the animal. A class "Animal Riddle" slide show is constructed from all the students' riddles.

ISTE NETS for Students— Standard 3: Technology Productivity Tools. Students use technology tools to enhance learning, increase productivity, and promote creativity. **Standard 4: Technology Communications Tools.** Students use a variety of media and formats to communicate information and ideas effectively to multiple audiences. Copyright © 2000, ISTE. All rights reserved.

Instructions

- During a study of animals, assign each student an animal to research.
- As a beginning, have them describe the appearance of the animal, what it eats, where it lives, where it belongs on the food chain, predators, etc.
- Have each student write a riddle with clues (information) about their animal without giving the identity. The last line of the clues should always be, "Who am I?"
- Ask each student to draw a picture of his or her animal and print its name below the animal.
- Put the picture of the animal and the clues that make up the riddle into a Kid Pix or PowerPoint slide show. One slide has the clues and the next slide has the picture (answer).
- Put all of the riddles into a class slide show of animal riddles.
- Present the slide show to your class.
- Send out invitations to other classes to view the show.

Lower Tech Level: Use Word to type the riddles. Have students draw pictures of their animals and bind all of them into a book.

Higher Tech Level: Create Web pages that are hyperlinked and publish the riddles on the web.

Teacher Education Connection: For Your Digital Portfolio: Create a similar slide show of people influencing education for a History of Education class.

---

[10] **Source:** Alice Potts, 2nd Grade Teacher, OK Elementary School, Wichita, KS.

Life Cycle of a Butterfly
Science
Beginning Tech Level for Grades K–5

Lesson Summary: Students observe (in person and using a webcam) and document (digital cameras) the life cycle of a butterfly (**NAS NRC 4**) to present a lesson (slide show) to students in their class and in other classes.

ISTE NETS for Students— Standard 4: Technology Communications Tools. Students use a variety of media and formats to communicate information and ideas effectively to multiple audiences. **Standard 5: Technology Research Tools.** Students use technology to locate, evaluate, and collect information from a variety of sources. Students use technology tools to process data and report results. Copyright © 2000, ISTE. All rights reserved.

Instructions

- Purchase a live butterfly kit, which will be shipped with cocoons and a hatching box with sides designed for viewing.
- Place the hatching box in a place where students may view the developments throughout the day.
- Take digital photos of the stages as they progress and have the students draw pictures of each stage using Kid Pix. A digital camera can be set to take hourly photos throughout the day, overnight, and on weekends.
- When the butterfly is about to emerge, use a webcam to take time-lapse photos to catch the process, step by step.
- Combine the children's drawings and the digital photos into a slide show, each slide showing drawings, photos, and words to describe the drawing.
- Present the "show" first to the class to critique. Make necessary modifications.
- Present the "show" to other classes in the building and/or parents.

Lower Tech Level: Use a standard camera to photograph the process.
Higher Tech Level: Create an animation with the time-lapse photos by having the slides of the Kid Pix slide show advance rapidly through these pictures.
Teacher Education Connection: For Your Digital Portfolio: Consider how time-lapse photography could be used in your methods coursework as you design experiences for students.

▷ *What is the Weather?*
Science
Intermediate Tech Level for Grades K–3

Lesson Summary: Students methodically predict, watch, and record information about the weather in their local area using the Internet to find the forecast for the week, digital cameras to record a daily picture, and the newspaper to find yesterday's weather (**NAS NRC 1, 5, 7**).

ISTE NETS for Students— Standard 3: Technology Productivity Tools. Students use productivity tools to collaborate in constructing technology-enhanced models, prepare publications, and produce other creative works. **Standard 5: Technology Research Tools.** Students use technology to locate, evaluate, and collect information from a variety of sources. Copyright © 2000, ISTE. All rights reserved.

Instructions

- Create a large wall Weather Calendar on which to record the predicted weather, a picture of the weather, and the actual weather as reported in the newspaper on the day following. Divide each cell of the calendar into three parts: Predicted, Picture, Reported.
- On Monday of each week, record the weekly forecast of the weather in your area. Try *The Weather Channel* (http://www.weather.com/).
- As part of the daily activities, at about the same time every day and from the same location, have students take a digital picture of the weather. Post the pictures on a calendar.
- Use the newspaper to record the weather from the previous day to see what actually happened on the Weather Calendar.
- At the end of the month compare and contrast the weather on the different days and make summary statements about the weather. Relate the information you have gathered to the seasons of fall, winter, spring, and summer.
- For those inquiring minds who seek other facts, make simple graphs for the month on which to record daily information from *The Weather Channel:* the wind direction, wind speed, dew point, temperature, humidity, visibility, and barometric pressure.

Lower Tech Level: Have students draw a picture of the weather rather than taking a digital picture.
Higher Tech Level: Record the information for the graphs in a spreadsheet program and print out several different pictorial representations.
Teacher Education Connection: For Your Digital Portfolio: Use a spreadsheet to keep track of information about your field experiences. Also include the amount of time you spend, the various types of activities, the grade level and/or subjects, and other demographic information about the school and students. Post in a variety of graphs.

Integrated Science Lessons

Heart Smart[11]

An Integrated Lesson for Science, Mathematics, and Physical Education
Intermediate Tech Level for Grades 7–12

Lesson Summary: Students learn the anatomy of the heart, about heart disease, and healthy hearts **(NASPE 4) (NAS NRC 7)**. They investigate family heart health history, statistics on heart disease, and research food choices that promote a healthy heart. They will participate in lifestyle activities **(NASPE 3)** that positively effect heart health, monitor heart rates, record data on spreadsheets, calculate target health rates **(NCTM)**, and make a personal health plan.

ISTE NETS for Student— Standard 5: Technology Research Tools. Students use technology to locate, evaluate, and collect information from a variety of sources. Students use technology tools to process data and report results. Copyright © 2000, ISTE. All rights reserved.

Instructions

- Introduce students to the anatomy of the heart, heart disease, and healthy hearts through texts, discussions, and Internet searches.
- Work with students to develop a set of questions to ask family members about family heart health history. Have students conduct the interviews.
- Have students wear a heart rate monitor for one week to record their heart rate at rest, during exercise and recovery, during and after eating, and during play and leisure and record their heart rate on a spreadsheet.
- Students calculate averages and target heart rate zone.
    - The **target heart rate** is a range of rates (beats per minute or bpm), expressed as a percentage of the maximum heart rate (MHR).
        - 220 (Average heart rate at birth) – 12 (age of student) = 208 Maximum heart rate (MHR).
        - The target heart-rate zone (THZ) is a percentage of the MHR. The goal of aerobic exercise is to exercise within the THZ. The American Heart Association recommends an exercise target heart rate ranging from 50 percent to 75 percent of the maximum heart rate. A simple formula for calculating THZ is:
        - MHR = 208 (for a 12-year-old). THZ = 208 x .50 = 104 and 208 x .75 = 156. THZ = 104 – 156 beats per minute.
- During physical education, students will choose one or more healthy heart aerobic activities and participate in stress- reducing activities such as yoga.
- Have students develop a personal health plan using the results of interviews, personal health history, and data collection on heart rate. Respect the privacy of these reports.

Lower Tech Level: Use the heart monitor only in class.

Higher Tech Level: Document and graph results over time.

Teacher Education Connection: For Your Digital Portfolio: Use a variety of tools to record personal health information. Note how to use these tools with students.

---

[11] **Source:** Dr. Colleen Evans-Fletcher and Dr. Vicki Worrell, Department of Kinesiology and Sport Studies, Wichita State University.

▶ *What's in a Cell?*[12]
An Integrated Science Lesson
Intermediate Tech Level for Grades 4–8

Lesson Summary: As part of a unit of study on cells (**NAS NCR 4, 6**), students use the Internet to gather information (**ELA 7**), a word processing program to summarize information, and a graphics program to draw and label cells (**ELA 4**).

ISTE NETS for Students— Standard 3: Technology Productivity Tools. Students use productivity tools to collaborate in constructing technology-enhanced models, prepare publications, and produce other creative works. **Standard 4: Technology Communications Tools.** Students use a variety of media and formats to communicate information and ideas effectively to multiple audiences. **Standard 5: Technology Research Tools.** Students use technology to locate, evaluate, and collect information from a variety of sources. Copyright © 2000, ISTE. All rights reserved.

Instructions

- Have students locate information about cells on the Internet and write a summary paragraph for each. Include information about (1) Chloroplast, (2) Cell Wall, (3) Vacuole, (4) Nucleus, and (5) Cell Membrane or "Plasma Membrane." Try *Rader's Kapili.com* (http://www.kapili.com/c/cell.html).
- Taking a virtual tour of a cell will allow students to better understand cells. *The Virtual Cell: Cell Biology* (http://personal.tmlp.com/jimr57/tour/cell/cell.htm)
- Examine the structure of plant, animal, and bacterial cells. (http://www.cellsalive.com/cells/3dcell.htm)
- After examination of several types of cells with their parts labeled, have students draw a cell using a drawing program.
- Label the cells organelles. Make sure they include (1) Chloroplast (in plants), (2) Cell Wall (in plants), (3) Cell Membrane, (4) Vacuole, (5) Nucleus, and (6) Cytoplasm.
- Merge the summary paragraphs with the labeled pictures to form the basis of a written project. The addition of an introductory paragraph and a conclusion help assess what students know about cells.

Lower Tech Level: Students use Internet and word processing, no graphics.

Higher Tech Level: Students use multimedia presentations to present information.

Teacher Education Connection: For Your Digital Portfolio: Gather information from the Internet about how technology might be used in classrooms. Draw an ideal setting for your content area. Label the parts.

---

[12] **Source:** Lori Trisler & Steve Smith, USD 259/Wichita State University: *Science Technology Integration Projects for Students* http://education.wichita.edu/m3/tips/science/fourth/4_s_classifying2.htm

▶ *All That Matter*
An Integrated Science Lesson
Beginning Tech Level for Grades K–2

Lesson Summary: Students collect objects from their environment and take digital pictures of each. Real objects are sorted according to their properties (**NAS NRC 3, 5**). The pictures are sorted within a software program, and labeled picture cards are matched to the real objects (**ELA 12**). Students make an *ABCs of Matter* book by putting the labeled pictures in alphabetical order (**ELA 4**).

ISTE NETS for Students— Standard 4: Technology Communications Tools. Students use a variety of media and formats to communicate information and ideas effectively to multiple audiences. **Standard 5: Technology Research Tools.** Students use technology to locate, evaluate, and collect information from a variety of sources. Students use technology tools to process data and report results. Copyright © 2000, ISTE. All rights reserved.

Instructions

- Investigate the properties of a few select items in the classroom (a shoe, a pencil, a book).
- Provide students with collection bags and rubber gloves so that they can each collect three things from the school grounds. Talk with them about safety in the collection of objects. Don't pick flowers, leaves, berries of live plants.
- Select two backgrounds to use as backdrops for the objects as you take a digital picture of each object.
- Save the pictures in two formats. The first is designed so that the picture and the label (for example: rock, twig, leaf, blade of grass) fit two to a page when printed (in color preferably). The second is such that just the pictures are saved, and small enough that many fit onto a single page.
- Set up several centers: (1) Sort the Objects. (2) Sort the Pictures. (3) Computer Sorting: Use the mouse to move the pictures into groups. Group and regroup the pictures. (4) Reading Center— make an ABC book using the pictures of the objects. (5) Writing Center— have labeled pictures and blank pieces of paper available so students can make their own picture-word cards.

Lower Tech Level: Use a regular camera and develop two prints.
Higher Tech Level: Set up a Web page with the collection of objects for other classes to see and share.
Teacher Education Connection: For Your Digital Portfolio: Take digital pictures of bulletin boards that you really like and want to remember. (Don't forget to ask permission first.)
Matter Matter Everywhere
http://education.wichita.edu/m3/tips/science/first/1_s_Matter.htm
Mr. Koday's Kids: Rocks and Minerals
http://www.ivyhall.district96.k12.il.us/4th/kkhp/RocksandMinerals/rocks.html

Biome Research and Comparison Project
An Integrated Multimedia Science Lesson
High Tech Level for Grades 6–12

Lesson Summary: Students study about animals using print and non-print resources including the Internet **(NAS NCR 4; ELA 7)**. A field trip to the zoo or nature center allows a multimedia photo and video shoot to gather photos, video, sound bites, and other informational data. The pieces are separated into three categories and edited to create a multimedia presentation, eventually linking all presentations together **(ELA 6, 8)**.

ISTE NETS for Students— Standard 4: Technology Communications Tools. Students use a variety of media and formats to communicate information and ideas effectively to multiple audiences. **Standard 5: Technology Research Tools.** Students use technology to locate, evaluate, and collect information from a variety of sources. Copyright © 2000, ISTE. All rights reserved.

Instructions

- Divide students into groups of 4–5 students each. Each group is assigned a different habitat or biome at the local zoo or nature center.
- Gather additional data from a variety of print and non-print sources such as books, videos, and the Internet. **(Check the school's Internet safe-use policies.)**
- Go on a multimedia video and photo shoot taking photos, video, sound bites, and gathering informational data.
- Edit the multimedia pieces into three categories, animals, plants, weather and geography.
- Use PhotoShop or other imaging software to size and adjust images.
- Use iMovie or other digital video editing software to create video clips.
- Use SoundEdit or other sound editing software to edit sound bytes and create voice-over narration.
- Create a multimedia presentation using all elements, hyperlinking the three categories together for a complete presentation on each biome.
- Have students show their work to the class comparing the different animals, plants, weather and geography.

Lower Tech Level: Students use only digital photos to document information found from other sources.

Teacher Education Connection: For Your Digital Portfolio: Prepare and teach a lesson. Document the lesson using photos, video, sound bites, and other informational data. Prepare a multimedia presentation.

Recycology: the Psychology of Recycling[13]
An Integrated Science Lesson
Adapt for Any Grade Level

Lesson Summary: Students set up an experiment (**NCSS 5**) to conduct at school and collaborate online to set it up at other schools around the country (**NCSS 8**) (**NAS NCR 3, 7**). Students compare anecdotal and cumulative data by e-mail and during prescheduled chatroom sessions.

ISTE NETS for Students— Standard 3: Technology Productivity Tools. Students use productivity tools to collaborate in constructing technology-enhanced models, prepare publications, and produce other creative works. **Standard 4: Technology Communications Tools.** Students use telecommunications to collaborate, publish, and interact with peers, experts, and other audiences. Copyright © 2000, ISTE. All rights reserved.

Instructions
- Set up a study. An example is included below.
- Contact a school(s) in another state and set up procedures for conducting the same experiment at their school. (Check the school's policies for online communication.)
- Set a schedule for sharing information by e-mail or other online forums.
- Report and analyze data separately and combined.
- Make recommendations to the school administration based on the results.

Example
- **Question:** How much do students use recycling boxes at school?
- **Baseline Data Collection:** Place the recycling boxes in the hall. Weigh them at the end of the first week as baseline data.
- **Intervention:** Determine and schedule intervention strategies beginning the second week and continuing for a predetermined amount of time. Examples: (1) put up recycling posters, (2) hold an assembly, (3) put an article in the bulletin or newspaper, (4) make daily announcements over the intercom, (4) have a lunch time rally, (5) establish challenges between floors or classes.
- **Data Collection:** Weigh/assess amount of recycled material each Friday.
- **Interpret Data:** Input all data in a spreadsheet and create charts or graphs (Tabletop or Graph Master) to analyze data, compare different variables, and share results.
- **Conclusions:** Take a final assessment and analyze the data. How much growth occurred over the month? At what point was the most "stuff" recycled? Discuss why you think what happened, happened.
- **Recommendations:** Make recommendations for increasing recycling to the school administration.

Lower Tech Level: Use e-mail only for the collaboration. Chart results by hand.
Higher Tech Level: Post a challenge on the Internet to other students to replicate the study and submit on a FileMaker Pro database that you establish.

---

[13] **Source:** Steve Witherspoon, IB Social Studies Teacher, East High School, Wichita, KS.

INTEGRATING ISTE STANDARDS INTO SOCIAL STUDIES

The **National Council for the Social Studies (NCSS)** provides leadership, service, and support for K–16 teachers and of history, geography, economics, political science, sociology, psychology, anthropology, and law-related education. "Social studies educators teach students the content knowledge, intellectual skills, and civic values necessary for fulfilling the duties of citizenship in a participatory democracy." (http://www.ncss.org/about/home.html)

For K–12 education, NCSS identifies 10 thematic strands that form the basis of the social studies standards which are more thoroughly explained in the Standards section of this book. Specific references to technology occur in several strands:

- Strand 3 (People, Places, and Environment): "Technological advances connect students at all levels to the world beyond their personal locations." (http://www.socialstudies.org/standards/2.3.html)
- Strand 7 (Production, Distribution, and Consumption): "Increasingly these decisions are global in scope and require systematic study of an interdependent world economy and the role of technology in economic decision-making." (http://www.socialstudies.org/standards/2.7.html)
- Strand 8 (Science, Technology, and Society): "Social studies programs should include experiences that provide for the study of relationships among science, technology, and society." Several specific examples for young, middle, and high school students appear within this strand. In addition, "Technology brings with it many questions:
  - Is new technology always better than that which it will replace?
  - What can we learn from the past about how new technologies result in broader social change, some of which is unanticipated?
  - How can we cope with the ever-increasing pace of change, perhaps even with the feeling that technology has gotten out of control?
  - How can we manage technology so that the greatest number of people benefit from it?
  - How can we preserve our fundamental values and beliefs in a world that is rapidly becoming one technology-linked village?"
  http://www.socialstudies.org/standards/2.8.html
- Strand 9 (Global Connections): "Through exposure to various media and first-hand experiences, young learners become aware of and are affected by events on a global scale." http://www.socialstudies.org/standards/2.9.html

The **ISTE NETS for Student Standards** that most align with the Social Studies area include **Standard 2: Social, Ethical, and Human Issues, and Standard 6: Technology Problem-solving and Decision-making Tools.**

Technology Tools for the Social Studies

Where in the World is Carmen Sandiego?
Where in the U.S.A. is Carmen Sandiego?
Carmen Sandiego's Great Chase Through Time
http://www.learningco.com/SubCategory.asp?CID=244
All three editions of Carmen Sandiego help students explore various areas of the social studies through interactive learning experiences. Newer editions include collections of essays, photos, and videos from National Geographic, Grolier's Encyclopedia, etc.

My First Amazing World Explorer 2.0
http://www.gzkidzone.com/gamesell/p14858.asp
Take an unforgettable trip to eight historical periods. Brings history to life and develops a sense of chronology. Children create a time journal to remind them of their travels.

GRASS GIS (Geographic Resources Analysis Support System)
http://www.baylor.edu/grass/
"GRASS GIS is an open source Geographical Information System (GIS) with raster, topological vector, image processing, and graphics production functionality that operates on various platforms through a graphical user interface and shell in X-Windows. Released under GNU General Public License (GPL)."

SimCity 3000 Unlimited
SimCity 3000 World Edition
http://simcity.ea.com/us/buildframes.phtml?guide/tips
Students develop an urban power by designing their own scenarios or use templates to customize a city (landscape, buildings, building sites, power, disasters, etc.). SimCity is supported by chats, contests, free downloads, and help.

GeoGenius USA
http://tukids.tucows.com/win95nt/9-12/preview/6520.html
Good graphical activities to familiarize one with states, capitals, regions, and general facts about the United States.

GeoGenius World
http://macinsearch.com/infomac2/education/yng/geo-genius-world.html
Click on a region to see the countries of that region up close. "Quiz Me" allows you to test your knowledge of the placement of the countries. The United States region tests your knowledge of the 50 states.

Social Studies Lessons

▶ *Community Health and Safety Workers*[14]
Social Studies
Beginning Tech Level for Grades K – 3

Lesson Summary: As part of a study on community health and safety workers (NCSS 3, 5), set up centers for the students to explore the roles these workers play and the tools they use. Students participate in these centers and a computer station that has two different WebQuests loaded for their exploration.

ISTE NETS for Students— Standard 5: Technology Research Tools. Students use technology to locate, evaluate, and collect information from a variety of sources. Copyright © 2000, ISTE. All rights reserved.

Instructions

- With the students, create a list of community health and safety workers. Have pictures ready of workers that could be on the list. While writing the list, discuss reasons why that worker would be on the list.
- Show the students the pictures. Group the pictures together by job. For example, a doctor, a nurse, and a dentist would go together, while an environmental worker would be in a group with a water quality inspector.
- Discuss workers in the following areas and the tools they use: health workers, environmental workers, safety workers
- Set up centers for students to extend their study of the workers: Art Center to make puppets of different workers to use: Dramatic Play Center (with clothes and tools to use), Puppet Center (for storytelling), Math Center (to sort tools and record measurements), Writing Center (for learning and using medical and emergency information), Computer Center (for completing the following two lessons). (Check the school's Internet safe-use policies.)
- *Computer Center.: Health and Environment Workers*
  http://education.wichita.edu/m3/tips/health/kdg/environment/webquestken.htm
- *Learn to be Safe at Home, School, and Play*
  http://education.wichita.edu/m3/tips/health/kdg/safety/webquestKs.htm

Lower Tech Level: Students can work in small groups with an adult at the computer center.
Higher Tech Level: Students can search safe sites for further information. Try *Web Pages for Kids about the Federal Government.*
http://www.hhs.gov/families/kids.htm
Teacher Education Connection: Construct a WebQuest associated with your content area. See *Some Thoughts about WebQuests* at
http://edweb.sdsu.edu/courses/EDTEC596/About_WebQuests.html

---

[14] **Source:** Joan Boles and Linda Miller, USD 259/Wichita State University: *Science Technology Integration Projects for Students.* http://education.wichita.edu/m3/tips/health/kdg/environment/lessonken.htm
http://education.wichita.edu/m3/tips/health/kdg/safety/lessonKs.htm

Exploring Cultures Around The World[15]
Social Studies
Intermediate Tech Level for Secondary Social Studies

Lesson Summary: Students search the Internet for sites to create a WebQuest as they find out where the five major religions are practiced (**NCSS 1 & 3**). Specific attention is paid to basic beliefs, rituals, geographic region, numbers, how it is practiced, and rituals in the same religion that are unique to different places in the world (**NCSS 9**).

ISTE NETS for Students— Standard 5: Technology Research Tools. Students use technology to locate, evaluate, and collect information from a variety of sources. Students use technology tools to process data and report results. Students evaluate and select new information resources and technological innovations based on the appropriateness for specific tasks. Copyright © 2000, ISTE. All rights reserved.

Instructions

- Review your school's policy about teaching and learning about religion. Remind students (and parents, if necessary) of the policies and the respect with which they must treat the information.
- **Check the school's Internet safe-use policies.**
- Review practices necessary to assure accuracy of information, especially on the Internet and to locate biases in the presentation of information.
- Divide class into five teams assigning each team a religion.
- Locate factual information from textbooks, library, and the web.
- Review copyright policies, citing print and non-print resources, and intellectual honesty. Use resources at http://www.thinkquest.org/resources/copyright.html and http://www.northwestern.edu/uacc/plagiary.html.
- As a class, discuss the information found and design a template for organizing information from each of the five religions into individual WebQuests linked to one class site.
- In order to design a WebQuest so that others can learn from the information, review Bernie Dodge's information and locate a template. http://edweb.sdsu.edu/courses/EDTEC596/About_WebQuests.html

Lower Tech Level: Use Word or other word processing programs to create the WebQuest. Word will automatically create hyperlinks from Web page addresses allowing the text document to become the "jumping off" point.
Higher Tech Level: Consider submitting the set of WebQuests to ThinkQuest or ThinkQuest Junior Contests (http://www.thinkquest.org/).

Teacher Education Connection: For Your Digital Portfolio: Use this process for examining different philosophies of education.

---

[15] **Source:** Steve Witherspoon, IB Social Studies Teacher, East High School, Wichita, KS.

▶ Expansion of the United States[16]
Social Studies
Intermediate Tech Level for Grades 7–12

Lesson Summary: In this American History lesson, students are required to add the appropriate states/territories that correlate to specific expansion events, such as the the Missouri Compromise or the Treaty of Guadalupe-Hildago, to existing maps (**NCGE 1, 6, 9**) presented on an electronic whiteboard.

ISTE NETS for Students— Standard 3: Technology Productivity Tools. Students use technology tools to enhance learning, increase productivity, and promote creativity. Students use productivity tools to collaborate in constructing technology-enhanced models, prepare publications, and produce other creative works. Copyright © 2000, ISTE. All rights reserved.

Instructions

- In preparation for this activity, make sure students have information about various expansion events in American History. (One way might be to have various small groups report on an assigned event.)
- Locate appropriate maps on mapping software or from the Internet.
  Geography with Matt Rosenberg
  http://geography.about.com/science/geography/?once=true&
  Discovery and Exploration
  http://memory.loc.gov/ammem/gmdhtml/dsxphome.html
- Post a map on an electronic whiteboard showing the United States before the expansion event.
- Ask students to draw the appropriate added states/territories that correlate with a specific expansion event and label the maps to show their understanding of the event, posting an appropriate legend.
- Check the students' "drawn" map against an "after-the-expansion-event" map.

Low Tech Level: Use overhead projector and transparencies. Save map graphics from the Internet or mapping software and print them out. Make transparencies from the printed copies.

Higher Tech Level: Put all the information from the research phase, existing map, and expansion map into an automated PowerPoint presentation supported by music, artwork, and pictures of the times.

Teacher Education Connection: For Your Digital Portfolio: Use your university as your home base. Map each extension into the community for each field experience in which you participate.

---

[16] **Source:** Steve Witherspoon, IB Social Studies Teacher, East High School, Wichita, KS.

Integrated Social Studies Lessons

▶ *The Effect of Topography and Climate On Production, Distribution, and Consumption of Goods and Services*[17]
An Integrated Social Studies Lesson
Intermediate Tech Level for Grades 7–12

Lesson Summary: Following a study of topography and climate maps (**NCGE 1, 3**), students select a country where there are topography and climate differences within that country. In the examination of those differences, they prepare a map of the country showing both the topography and the climate. A legend will provide icons to indicate the natural resources and the production, distribution, and consumption of goods and services in each region (**NCGE 11; NCSS 2, 7**). A final report will explain the project, summarize the findings, and project what will happen or need to happen (**NCGE 18**).

ISTE NETS for Students— Standard 5: Technology Research Tools. Students use technology to locate, evaluate, and collect information from a variety of sources. Students use technology tools to process data and report results. Copyright © 2000, ISTE. All rights reserved.

Instructions
- **Check the school's Internet safe-use policies.**
- Extend the study of topographic maps and climate maps to learn more about these maps, their symbols, and how to read them with online sources: *Matt Rosenberg's Topographic Maps* or *Koppen's Climate Map*. (See other online resources later in the book.)
- Divide the class into groups and assign each group a different region of the selected country.
- Using textbooks, the library, and the Internet, gather information and create a topographical and climate map for each region. Use map-making software to complete the maps.
- Mark each region with the topography, climate, and natural resources discovered in the research phase.
- Explore the country's production, distribution, and consumption of goods and services.
- Present the projects in writing to the teacher or as presentations to the class.
- Compare and contrast all maps. What are the similarities and differences? What correlations are evident? What do the results suggest about political and economic interaction among these regions?

Lower Tech Level: Hand draw the maps from outlines provided by the teacher.
Higher Tech Level: Prepare hypermedia presentations to report findings. Post all to the Internet.
Teacher Education Connection: For Your Digital Portfolio: Locate and use social, political, and population maps to teach about art, music, sports, religions.

---

[17] **Source:** Steve Witherspoon, IB Social Studies Teacher, East High School, Wichita, KS.

Behavior Patterns in Sociological Phenomena[18]
An Integrated Social Studies Lesson
Intermediate Level Tech Skill for Grades 9–12

Lesson Summary: Students gather information from the archives of several newspapers for examples of specific sociological phenomena (mass weddings, town festivals/celebrations, road rage, suburban growth). Students organize the information and place the events on a map to determine patterns of behavior for various regions of the country/world (**NCSS 3, 4, 5; NCGE 10**).

ISTE NETS for Students—Standard 5: Technology Research Tools. Students use technology to locate, evaluate, and collect information from a variety of sources. Students use technology tools to process data and report results. Copyright © 2000, ISTE. All rights reserved.

Instructions

- **Check the school's Internet safe-use policies.**
- Assign small groups of students one specific sociological phenomenon (mass weddings, town festivals/celebrations, etc.).
- Search for information about these issues in local newspapers.
- Provide Internet access to online newspapers. Try the Internet Public Library Online Newspapers for a comprehensive listing (http://www.ipl.org/reading/news/)
- Summarize the information located at each site, noting the time and location of the article and the reference information necessary for citing information from newspapers or online newspapers.
- Mark the locations of the events on a digital world map and label each with a title. Have students create theories as to why certain phenomena occur in certain regions of the world more frequently.
- Write a brief report to include an introduction, information from a variety of sources, a graphic of the marked map, and summary information (compiling results, interpretation, and reflection).

Lower Tech Level: Use paper maps to mark locations. Rather than inserting a graphic of the map in the paper, attach a scanned copy to the report.
Higher Tech Level: Use Tom Snyder's timeline software, a spreadsheet, or word processing software to place these same events on a timeline. By looking at chronological trends, what different perspective are evident?
Teacher Education Connection: For Your Digital Portfolio: Locate and use social, political, and population maps to teach about art, music, sports, religions.

---

[18] **Source:** Steve Witherspoon, IB Social Studies Teacher, East High School, Wichita, KS.

My Culture and Yours[19]
An Integrated Social Studies Lesson
Intermediate Tech Level for All Grades

Lesson Summary: In this world history lesson, students use real-time chats, e-mail, or discussion groups with students in another school (keypals) or in another country to learn about their respective countries (**NCGE 1**) and cultures (**NCSS 1, 3, 5, 9**) while providing information about their own.

ISTE NETS for Students— Standard 4: Technology Communications Tools. Students use telecommunications to collaborate, publish, and interact with peers, experts, and other audiences. Students use a variety of media and formats to communicate information and ideas effectively to multiple audiences. Copyright © 2000, ISTE. All rights reserved.

Instructions
- **Check the school's Internet safe-use policies for online communication.**
- Locate a classroom of e-mail pals from a reliable Internet source. (A Yahoo search of e-pals Web pages is a good beginning.)
- Determine the desired method of communication tool (e-mail, live chat, discussion group) and the grouping structure (individual, small group, whole group). (For additional information, see *Y!GeoCities Chat Etiquette* online at http://www.geocities.com/SouthBeach/Breakers/5257/Chatet.htm)
- Make initial contact with the teacher of the other class to determine the process to be used.
- Study about the area of the world where the e-pals live.
- Generate a list of questions that students would like to ask the other students.
- Discuss Netiquette (For more information, see *Netiquette Primer* http://jade.wabash.edu/wabnet/info/netiquet.htm.)
- Have students formulate written answers to the questions themselves.
- Establish connections with the e-pals.
- Ask and respond appropriately to questions. Record the responses. Bring appropriate closure to the conversation(s).
- Compare and contrast all responses.

Low Tech Level: Use the postal service, sending letters and videotapes.
High Tech Level: Use webcams, NetMeeting, or other video conferencing software instead of e-mail, live chats, and online discussion.
Teacher Education Connection: For Your Digital Portfolio: Correspond online with a preservice teacher at a place geographically and culturally different from yours to compare and contrast school experiences.

---

[19] **Source:** Steve Witherspoon, IB Social Studies Teacher, East High School, Wichita, KS.

▶ Perspectives on History
An Integrated Social Studies Lesson
Beginning Tech Level Lower Grades–Intermediate Tech Level for Upper Grades

Lesson Summary: Younger students learn about an historical event (**NCSS 5**) by communicating with older students online (**ELA 1, 5, 12**).

ISTE NETS for Students— Standard 4: Technology Communications Tools. Students use telecommunications to collaborate, publish, and interact with peers, experts, and other audiences. Students use a variety of media and formats to communicate information and ideas effectively to multiple audiences. **Standard 5: Technology Research Tools.** Students use technology to locate, evaluate, and collect information from a variety of sources. Copyright © 2000, ISTE. All rights reserved.

Instructions

- **Check your schools Internet safe-use policies for online communication.**
- This activity requires a class of younger and older students. At least three grade levels should be between the two classes. Locate a second teacher online who has a group of either younger or older students, and either another classroom in your building, another classroom in your district, or a more distant one.
- Choose one of three strategies.
    - Have both groups of students read about an historical event such as the discovery of America or Paul Revere's ride. Have younger students draw their perspective of the event using a graphics program such as Kid Pix or scan their drawings and send them to the older group. Using the drawings, the older group writes captions for them and creates a Web page to explain the event. The younger students can then safely read about the event online.
    - Have older students take roles such as Columbus, Magellan, George Washington, or Paul Revere and answer students' questions as if they were that person. Instruct younger students to ask questions such as, "What did it feel like to ride through the night yelling, 'The British are coming?' "
    - Using e-mail, have the younger students write letters to the older class asking questions about the event and the people involved. After researching the queries, the older class must respond by e-mail to answer the questions.

Lower Tech Level: Answer only by e-mail. Form the answers in picture books.
Higher Tech Level: Make a slide show or use clay animation to tell the story.
Teacher Education Connection: For Your Digital Portfolio: Contact a practicing teacher who is willing to respond to questions about how they implement things you are learning in your course work.

▶ Around the World: Transportation
An Integrated Social Studies Lesson
Beginning Tech Level for Grades 4–8

Lesson Summary: Within the study of world history or world geography, students research the various types of transportation used on each of the inhabited continents of the world (**NCSS 5, 7**) and the costs associated with each (**NCTM**).

ISTE NETS for Students— Standard 4: Technology Communications Tools. Students use a variety of media and formats to communicate information and ideas effectively to multiple audiences. **Standard 5: Technology Research Tools.** Students use technology to locate, evaluate, and collect information from a variety of sources. Students use technology tools to process data and report results. Copyright © 2000, ISTE. All rights reserved.

Instructions

- Associated with a unit of study in world history or world geography, group students and have them use the Internet and library resources to find modes of transportation for one of the inhabited continents of the world, a different continent per group.
- Once modes of transportation are identified, costs associated with those methods of transportation are identified.
- Students insert information into a table that identifies the mode of transportation and the cost.
- Each group presents their results to the rest of the class, summarizing the process they used to locate the information and the information that they found.
- Tables can be posted on a world map bulletin board.
- Future assignments can focus on foods, clothing, goods, and resources.

Lower Tech Level: Students locate the information in the library and in encyclopedias and create the graph by hand.

Higher Tech Level: Students create a database with information about the country, the type of transportation, the associated costs, which allows the sorting of information by type, and continent, and cost.

Teacher Education Connection: For Your Digital Portfolio: Create a database of the various configurations of schools (PreK–16) in several different places in your state, noting vacancies in the schools where you would consider teaching. For example: Wichita Public School District has schools of the following configurations: P–K, P–2, P–5, K–5, 6–8, 9–12, 13–16, and virtual school for home-schooled students.

Create a City
An Integrated Social Studies Lesson
Beginning Tech Level for Grades K – 3

Lesson Summary: Students share knowledge about their community as they develop a model community of their own **(NCSS 3, 5)**. Supported by SimCity or City Builder and limited by a 4-foot x 8-foot space, students can decide how best to organize and map their city with limited resources **(NCGE 1, 3) (NCEE 1)**.

ISTE NETS for Students— Standard 6: Technology Problem-solving and Decision-making Tools: Students use technology resources for solving problems and making informed decisions. Copyright © 2000, ISTE. All rights reserved.

Instructions

- Provide each student with a shoebox and the task of designing their own room. (Materials needed for the project include wallpaper scraps, carpet scraps, glue, crayons, scissors, balsa wood scraps, etc.) Students design their shoebox room, using wallpaper and carpet scraps, drawing pictures for the walls, and constructing furniture from balsa wood scraps.
- Use a 4' x 8' piece of plywood on which to place student houses. Arrange the rooms (houses) in any way students wish. As they begin to place their boxes on the city, other needs will emerge (business, recreation, industry, transportation, emergency/medical, etc.)
- Using a city building program (SimCity or City Builder) or drawing program, have students draw a plan for their city.
- Photograph the layout and post the photograph with the printout near the actual "city."
- Change the physical city weekly for several weeks, challenging students to look for different and better ways to accomplish their goals. Draw and photograph each.
- Compare and contrast all the different city shapes and determine the best plans.
- Post the various photographs and computer-generated layouts of the city next to the actual model and leave it for parents to view at conferences or Open House.

Lower Tech Level: Use a graphics function of a word processing or a graphics program to replicate the city the students build. Label the parts.
Higher Tech Level: Plan the city first using SimCity or City Builder and then construct it.
Teacher Education Connection: For Your Digital Portfolio: Draw maps of the various classrooms you visit, noting technology in each. Plan your own ideal classroom.

All About Me Timeline
An Integrated Social Studies Lesson
Beginning Tech Level for Grades K–3

Lesson Summary: Younger students learn about time in terms of themselves—what I am doing, what I did yesterday (or before), and what I will do next (or tomorrow). This lesson provides an opportunity for a family homework project and the construction of timelines (**NCTM**) of events in children's lives to compare and contrast (**NCSS 2, 4**).

ISTE NETS for Students—Standard 5: Technology Research Tools. Students use technology tools to process data and report results. Copyright © 2000, ISTE. All rights reserved.

Instructions

- In helping them learn about time and the representation of events, assign families the responsibility of entering data in sequential order for a family homework assignment. As part of this "All About Me" homework, include date of birth, sitting, crawling, walking, first tooth, birth of siblings. (Be sensitive for issues like adoption, moves, deaths, broken bones, hospital visits, etc.)
- Connect this assignment with books about events in children's lives as well as similarities and differences in children.
- Work with students to enter the information onto a timeline (try Timeliner 5.0), leaving a standard space for each month so that when all timelines are posted the years and months line up. Save each individual timeline and continue adding special events throughout the year.
- Compare and contrast the information on the set of printed timelines looking for similarities, differences, and unique qualities of the students.
- Roll the timelines into a scroll, tie with a ribbon, and send home for Mother's or Father's Day.

Lower Tech Level: Draw the timeline, using different colors for different years or decades.

Higher Tech Level: Have parents send photographs with the events. Scan the pictures into the timeline.

Teacher Education Connection: For Your Digital Portfolio: Complete timelines for various educational themes (laws, people, types of schools, child-rearing practices, social ills) keeping a standard measurement for each decade from 1600–present day. Compare and contrast the events. Follow themes through the decades and centuries.

SEVEN STEPS TO RESPONSIBLE SOFTWARE SELECTION
May 1995   EDO-IR-95-6

This ERIC Digest is based on a manuscript "Seven Steps to Responsible Software Selection" submitted to ERIC/IT by P. Kenneth Komoski of The Educational Products Information Exchange (EPIE) and was prepared by Eric Plotnick, Assistant Director, ERIC Clearinghouse on Information & Technology. (Note: This ERIC Digest document is in the public domain and may be freely reproduced and disseminated.)

In the early 1980s, relatively inexpensive microcomputers came on the market, the personal computer was selected *Time* magazine's "man (machine) of the year," and school administrators rushed to buy early generation Apple, TRS-80, Commodore, or similar computers for their schools. Educational software was limited, and what little there was consisted mostly of "drill and practice" electronic worksheets. Teachers often selected software from catalogs, choosing almost any software that remotely touched on the subjects they were teaching. Often they were disappointed when the software arrived. Almost fifteen years later, microcomputers in schools are no longer a novelty, but contribute significantly in the learning process, and software selection is taken as seriously as the selection of textbooks. This Digest will outline a seven-step process for responsible software selection.

Step 1. Analyze Needs

The responsible teacher (or materials selection committee) should first determine whether or not the computer is the appropriate medium to use to satisfy particular instructional goals and objectives. There is always the possibility that a careful needs analysis will result in a decision to use some other teaching-learning strategy.

Needs and Goals. A need is the difference between "where we are now" (e.g. 60% of the students in the ninth grade score above minimum competence on the state science test) and "where we would like to be" (e.g. 90% of the students in ninth grade score above minimum competence on the state science test). "Where we would like to be" is another way of defining a goal.

Objectives. An objective describes "where we would like to be" in more specific terms (e.g. 90% of all ninth grade students will exceed the minimum level of competence on the state competency test administered in the second semester of ninth grade). Objectives must include conditions under which the desired behavior will be demonstrated and the criteria for measuring that behavior.

Educational objectives help us respond to needs by breaking them down into attainable steps, making it easier to get from "where we are now" to "where we would like to be." The educational objective stated above is a "terminal" objective which must be broken down into a series of "enabling" objectives (e.g. By October 31, 1995, all ninth grade students will be able to correctly identify at least five out of seven minerals when shown them by the teacher.) Enabling objectives identify specifically what behavior we would like the student to demonstrate. For each enabling objective, the teacher (or materials selection committee) should brainstorm alternative learning methods for achieving that objective— direct student with teacher interaction, self-instruction workbook, videotape, computer assisted instruction, etc.

After considering the benefits and constraints of each learning method, the teacher (or materials selection committee) should be able to make an informed decision about which medium or combination of media will satisfy the identified needs, goals, and objectives.

Step 2. Specify Requirements

If a careful needs analysis determines that computer assisted instruction is one of the methods that will be used to meet identified instructional objectives, the teacher (or materials selection committee) should then specify the requirements for the computer software. Factors to consider in specifying requirements for software include: compatibility with available hardware; cost (Will the school need multiple copies of the software? Will a site license be necessary?); user friendliness; level of interaction desired; adequacy of documentation; access to technical support via toll-free number; and of course, direct correlation with the instructional objectives and curriculum requirements identified in the needs analysis. Ellsworth and Hedley (1993) suggest that educators should apply the following criteria within the context of their objectives and the students' needs: content; instructional presentation; demands placed on the learner; technical features; and documentation and management features.

Step 3. Identify Promising Software

If requirements are specified in detail, the teacher (or materials selection committee) will have a good head start when it comes to identifying promising software. There are many ways to identify promising software, and the responsible selector should use as many of them as possible. Catalogs still remain an important source for descriptions of software. Most district level educational communications/media centers are on catalog mailing lists from virtually all software producers and wholesalers. Software is advertised, described, and often reviewed in magazines and journals found in school, university, and public libraries. The Educational Products Information Exchange (EPIE) produces The Educational Software Selector (TESS), a database containing descriptions and reviews of thousands of currently published educational software programs.

Teachers who have access to the Internet can find out about software from other teachers by joining a listserv. Posting a question such as, "I am an eighth grade science teacher and I am looking for interactive software for a PC environment that will teach my students how to . . . " is likely to bring dozens of responses. Many listservs are archived on the AskERIC Virtual Library gopher (gopher ericir.syr.edu) or WWW site (http://ericir.syr.edu). Directions for joining a listserv may be found in the archives, or e-mail AskERIC@ericir.syr.edu for more information on listservs.

The above are but a few sources for identifying promising software. The more precisely the requirements are specified in Step 2, the easier it will be to screen out those products that are least likely to meet the user's specifications and the easier it will be to focus on more promising products.

Step 4. Read Relevant Reviews

After a list of promising software has been identified (using the suggestions outlined in Step 3), the teacher (or materials selection committee) may be able to narrow or expand the list by reading relevant software reviews. It is very important to realize, however, that reading reviews should not take the place of previewing, described in Step 5. Software reviews may be found in educational journals, some of which may be identified by searching the ERIC database using appropriate descriptors (e.g. software, selection, evaluation, elementary, secondary). For example, Heyboer and Mayo, in the January 1993 issue of *Teacher Magazine*, describe 12 computer software programs available for elementary and secondary math and science classes. Evaluation services such as EPIE, subscribed to by many school and public libraries, provide a database of selected software evaluations and reviews. A visit to the library is an important part of responsible software selection. Keep Step 1 (Analyze Needs) and Step 2 (Specify Requirements) in mind as you read the reviews. It is also important to note the audience upon which the review is based. A software program may have received a poor review because it was tested with a different audience than the one you have in mind. Reviews are important screening tools when used as part of the entire selection process.

Step 5. Preview Software

The most effective way to judge whether software is appropriate or not is to observe students as they interact with the program. Are the educational objectives achieved when the student uses the program? The responsible teacher should not purchase software without previewing it with his or her own students. Preview as many programs as you can find that appear to meet your selection criteria. Some software vendors will allow free preview of an entire program. Some vendors will provide a free demonstration disk containing a subset of a larger program. Some vendors will not allow preview without a purchase order, but will allow the teacher to return the program within a specified time limit with no financial obligation. In some situations, a teacher may be able to borrow a program from another teacher for preview purposes. As a general rule, if there is no way to preview software with your own students— avoid that software.

Step 6. Make Recommendations

After potential software has been previewed, it is time to make recommendations for purchase. The responsible software selector should be able

- To select the most desirable software after a systematic evaluation of all alternatives in terms of educational objectives and constraints;
- To establish a quantitative method for rating each alternative against the selection criteria established in Step 2;
- To evaluate the relative importance of each selection criterion (ie. previewing should probably be rated relatively high in importance); and
- To create a written record outlining the reasons why a piece of software is recommended or not recommended for purchase.

For software that is recommended for purchase, teachers should include suggestions for optimal use that might have become apparent during the preview period. The written record, including the quantitative rating scale and the selection criteria, should be kept on file for future reference.

Step 7. Get Post-Use Feedback

After software is purchased and used with students, it is important for the teacher to determine the conformance or discrepancy between all of the enabling objectives specified in Step 1 and the student performance actually obtained using the chosen computer software. The teacher should keep records on the relative extent to which each objective is met or not met. Objectives not met may be addressed by some other software program or by another teaching/learning method. Post-use feedback can be a significant help to a school's systematic process of software selection, purchase and use. The accumulation of user feedback, including anecdotal experience on the part of both teachers and students, will naturally serve to improve future needs analyses (Step 1) and all succeeding steps in a constantly improving software selection process.

References

Best, A. & Mathis, J. (Eds.). (1993*). The 1993–94 educational software preview guide.* Educational Software Evaluation Consortium. Eugene, OR: International Society for Technology in Education. (ED 366 331)

Broderick, B. & Caverly, D.C. (1993). Techtalk: Choosing and purchasing software. *Journal of Developmental Education, 17*(1), 40–41. (EJ 469 271)

DeLaurentiis, E. C. (1993). *How to recognize excellent educational software.* New York: Lifelong Software, Inc. (ED 355 932)

Ellsworth, N. J. & Hedley, C. N. (1993). What's new in software? Selecting software for student use. *Reading and Writing Quarterly: Overcoming Learning Difficulties, 9*(2), 207–211. (EJ 465 250)

Heyboer, K. & Mayo, C. (1993). Software to swear by. *Teacher Magazine, 4*(4), 22–23. (EJ 461 943)

ONLINE RESOURCES

The Web seems to be a living breathing entity. Web sites are posted and deleted, organized and reorganized, named and renamed. At the time of publication these links were correct. If they are not live, search for the title of the Web site.

Comprehensive Lesson Plan Sites

Apple Learning Interchange
http://ali.apple.com/

Ask ERIC Lesson Plans
http://ericir.syr.edu/Virtual/Lessons/

Awesome Library K–12 Education Directory
http://www.neat-schoolhouse.org/awesome.html

Blue Web'n
http://www.kn.pacbell.com/wired/bluewebn/

The Busy Teacher's Website
http://www.ceismc.gatech.edu/busyt/homepg.htm

Canada's Schoolnet Learning Resources
http://www.schoolnet.ca/home/e/resources/

Classroom Connect's Connected Teacher
http://www.connectedteacher.com/home.asp

Discovery School
http://school.discovery.com/

Federal Resources for Educational Excellence
http://www.ed.gov/free/

Gateway to Educational Materials
http://www.thegateway.org/

Infomine
http://infomine.ucr.edu/search/k12search.phtml

Innovative Classroom
http://www.innovativeclassroom.com/

Innovative Teaching
http://www.surfaquarium.com/it.htm

The Journal Educator's Road Map to the Internet
http://www.thejournal.com/features/rdmap/

Kathy Schrock's Guide for Educators
http://school.discovery.com/schrockguide/

Lesson Plan Archives
http://www.rmcdenver.com/useguide/lessons/design.htm?#lessons

Lesson Plans and Teaching Strategies
http://www.csun.edu/~hcedu013/plans.html

The Library in the Sky
http://www.nwrel.org/sky/

Lightspan
http://www.lightspan.com/

Links for K–12 Teachers
http://www.memphis-schools.k12.tn.us/admin/tlapages/k12links.htm

MiddleWeb
http://www.middleweb.com/Links.html

Net Day Compass
http://www.netdaycompass.org/

PBS TeacherSource
http://www.pbs.org/teachersource/

School.Net— Best Links
http://k12.school.net/links

The School Page
http://www.eyesoftime.com/teacher/index.htm

Smithsonian Institution
http://www.si.edu/

TeachNet Lesson Ideas
http://www.teachnet.com/lesson/index.html

Search Engines

All the Web	http://alltheweb.com/
AltaVista	http://www.AltaVista.com/
Britannica.com	http://www2.britannica.com/
Direct Hit	http://www.directhit.com/
Dogpile	http://www.Dogpile.com/
Excite	http://www.Excite.com/education/
Go.com	http://www.go.com/
Google	http://www.google.com/
HotBot	http://hotbot.lycos.com/
Ixquick	http://www.ixquick.com
Lycos	http://www.lycos.com/
Magellan	http://magellan.excite.com/
Metacrawler	http://www.metacrawler.com/
NBCi	http://www.nbci.com/
Northern Light	http://www.northernlight.com/
Search.com	http://www.search.com/
Searchopolis	http://www.searchopolis.com/
Webcrawler	http://www.Webcrawler.com/
Yahoo	http://www.yahoo.com/

Search Engines for Students

AOL Net Find: Kids Only	http://www.aol.com/netfind/kids/
Ask Jeeves for Kids	http://www.ajkids.com/
Family Friendly Search	http://www.familyfriendlysearch.com/
Kids Click!	http://sunsite.berkeley.edu/KidsClick!/
Kid's Edge	http://www.kidsedge.com/
Yahooligans	http://www.yahooligans.com

Web Site Evaluation

Blue Web'n Site Evaluation Rubric
http://www.kn.pacbell.com/wired/bluewebn/rubric.html

The ABCs of Web Site Evaluation
http://kathyschrock.net/abceval/

The ABCs of Web Site Evaluation:
Teaching Media Literacy in the Age of the Internet
http://www.connectedteacher.com/newsletter/abcs.asp

Evaluating Websites for Curriculum Use
http://www.germantownacademy.org/Academics/US/Library/Internet/
  Evaluation/teacher.htm

WWW Cyberguides
http://www.cyberbee.com/guide1.html

WebQuest Collections

Bernie Dodge's Graduate Student's WebQuests
http://www.lfelem.lfc.edu/tech/DuBose/webquest/wq.html

Bernie Dodge WebQuests
http://www.macomb.k12.mi.us/wq/webqindx.htm

Filamentality WebQuest Collection
http://www.kn.pacbell.com/wired/fil/

Memphis City Schools WebQuest Collection
http://www.memphis-schools.k12.tn.us/admin/tlapages/web_que.htm

Science Centered WebQuests
http://horizon.nmsu.edu/ddl/ddllessongrid.html

TrackStar WebQuest Collection
http://trackstar.hprtec.org/

Online Resources for English/Language Arts

Online English/Language Arts Content

Biographies http://www.biography.com
Brief biographical information is provided for thousands of people. Links to connected sites. Listings of works or major deeds are included.

Great Books On-line http://www.bartleby.com/
An Internet publisher of literature, reference, and verse.

Gutenberg Project http://www.promo.net/pg/
This project makes information available to the general public in forms a vast majority of people can easily read, use, quote, and search.

Internet Public Library: Youth Division http://www.ipl.org/youth/
This site provides information on a variety of topics.

The Online Books Page http://www.digital.library.upenn.edu/books/
This Web site facilitates access to books that are freely readable over the Internet and aims to encourage the development of such on-line books.

On-line English Grammar
http://www.edunet.com/english/grammar/index.cfm
Terms are defined, examples are given, and use is explained.

Online ELA Lesson Plans

Awesome Library: English and Language Arts
http://www.awesomelibrary.org/englishg.html
Links to lesson plans on literature, drama, bilingual education, and public speaking.

Language Arts http://www.rsf.k12.ca.us/Subjects/La.html
Literature, writing, journalism, poetry, mechanics sites are linked here.

Language Arts Web Links
http://cw.prenhall.com/bookbind/pubbooks/methods-cluster/chapter4/deluxe.html

National Council of Teachers of English http://www.ncte.org/teach/
A searchable site for teaching ideas in ESL, journalism, literature, reading, technology, writing, vocabulary

PBS Teachers Source http://www.pbs.org/teachersource/arts_lit.htm
A searchable index of lesson plans for language arts.

SCORE California http://www.sdcoe.k12.ca.us/score/cy68.html
Lesson plans are provided for several adolescent literature and young adult books.

Online Resources for Math

Online Math Content

Figure This: Math Challenges for Families http://www.figurethis.org/
Funded by NSF and US Department of Education, copyrights held by NCTM:
Several challenging math activities to select from in English and Spanish.

MASTER Tools: Modeling and Simulation Tools for Education Reform
http://www.shodor.org/master/
MASTER Tools are designed to be "interactive tools and simulation environments
that enable and encourage exploration and discovery through observation,
conjecture, and modeling activities."

Ms. Lindquist: The Tutor http://www.algebratutor.org/
An interactive tutor created by Carnegie Mellon University

themathlab.com
http://www.themathlab.com/
An interactive math site for middle and high school students

Topics in Math http://archives.math.utk.edu/topics/
An extensive searchable webliography of online math resources

Online Math Lesson Plans

*The Eisenhower National Clearinghouse for Mathematics and Science
Education (ENC)* http://www.enc.org/
The ENC acquires and catalogs K–12 mathematics and science resources.

Explorer http://unite.ukans.edu/
Educational resources for K–12 mathematics and science education.

The Math Forum http://forum.swarthmore.edu/
A comprehensive math site which includes Ask Dr. Math, Internet Newsletter,
Problems of the Week in several areas, Teacher2Teacher, Web Units and Lesson
Plans.

Math Web Links
cw.prenhall.com/bookbind/pubbooks/methods-cluster/chapter4/deluxe.html

MWREL's Library in the Sky Math Lessons
http://www.nwrel.org/sky/department.asp?ID=0&d=7
Nearly 100 lessons provided in 10 categories.

ThinkQuest http://www.thinkquest.org/
Search ThinkQuest for math lessons.

Online Resources for Science

Online Science Content
Astronomy Picture of the Day
http://antwrp.gsfc.nasa.gov/apod/astropix.html

Health, Science, Technology, Animation   http://www.brainpop.com/

Human Body Adventure
http://vilenski.com/science/humanbody/hb_html/map.html

NASA Education Program, Star Child, Why Files
http://education.nasa.gov/

National Institute of Environmental Health Sciences
http://www.niehs.nih.gov/kids/links.htm

Learning Web at the US Geological Survey
http://www.usgs.gov/education/

Science Internet Education Resources Index
http://cl.k12.md.us/EdResources/ScienceIndex.html

TryScience Online Experiments
http://www.tryscience.org/exp_firstframesa.html

Online Science Lesson Plans
Eisenhower National Clearinghouse   http://www.enc.org

Elementary Science Resources-1998. Elementary Activities
http://eisen.kcmetro.cc.mo.us/98/elemsci.htm

Frank Potter's Science Gems   http://www.sciencegems.com/

Lawrence Hall of Science Berkeley   http://www.lhs.berkeley.edu/

NSTA   http://www.nsta.org/onlineresources/site/

Science Internet Education Resources Index
http://cl.k12.md.us/EdResources/ScienceIndex.html

Science Web Links
cw.prenhall.com/bookbind/pubbooks/methods-cluster/chapter4/deluxe.html

Sky and Telescope   http://www.skypub.com/

StarDate Online   http://stardate.utexas.edu/

World Wide Planetarium Directory   http://www.lochness.com/

Online Resources for Social Studies

Online Social Studies Content

American Memory http://lcWeb2.loc.gov/
Exemplar of an online digital library with historical photographs

BBC Online History http://www.bbc.co.uk/history
Search for a topic in history and get the British perspective.

Biographies http://www.biography.com

Geographic Learning Site (US Department of State)
http://geography.state.gov/htmls/teacher.html

Geography with Matt Rosenberg (maps, quizzes, discussion, info)
http://geography.about.com/science/geography/?once=true&

GeoResources (UK) http://www.georesources.co.uk/index.htm
Contains links, virtual fieldwork, case studies, outline maps, weather data, etc.

History Matters http://historymatters.gmu.edu/search.taf
A massive searchable index of primary source documents.

National Geographic for Kids http://www.nationalgeographic.com/kids/

US Geological Survey Department of the Interior
http://ask.usgs.gov/education.html

Valley of the Shadow http://jefferson.village.virginia.edu/vshadow2/
Plans with linked primary sources to study of Civil War for Grade 7–college.

Whitehouse on Museums
http://www.whitehouse.gov/government/handbook/text/museum.html

Online Social Studies Lesson Plans

American's Freedom Documents
http://www.education-world.com/a_lesson/lesson190.shtml

Central Intelligence Agency's Homepage for Kids
http://www.odci.gov/cia/ciakids/index.html

The National Geography Standards (with lesson plans)
http://www.eloff.com/~poster_ed/NGSstds.html

Teaching Geography Through the Internet
http://www.oranim.macam98.ac.il/geo/ndx_geo.html

SOFTWARE

Throughout the book we've mentioned many software titles. Keeping up with the newest editions and upgrades is a big job. The most important thing is to choose a few basic pieces and learn them well so that they can become powerful tools for you and your students. This is a list of a few of our favorites in several categories. As more and more content is delivered on the Internet, the most important classroom software will be (1) an Internet browser; (2) word processing, spreadsheet, and database tools; and (3) multimedia and graphics software.

Applications/Productivity
- Microsoft Office (Word, Excel, PowerPoint, FrontPage, Access)
  Microsoft
- Inspiration/Kidspiration
  Inspiration Software, Inc.
- FileMaker Pro
  FileMaker

Teacher Tools
- Grade Machine
  Misty City Software, Inc.
- School Font Collection
  Visions
- FoolProof
  SmartStuff Software

Creativity and Thinking
- Stagecast Creator
  The Learning Company
- Logical Journey of the Zoombinis
  The Learning Company
- MicroWorlds
  LCSI

Graphics and Multimedia
- iMovie
  Apple
- Adobe PhotoShop
  Adobe
- HyperStudio
  Knowledge Adventure
- Kid Pix Studio Deluxe
  The Learning Company

Early Childhood

- Sammy's Science House
  Edmark
- Reader Rabbit's Learn To Read
  The Learning Company
- Living Books
  The Learning Company

Math

- The Tabletop Jr. and Sr.
  TERC
- The Graph Club or Graph Masters
  Tom Snyder Productions
- Geometer's Sketchpad
  Key Curriculum Press
- Green Globs and Graphing Equations
  Sunburst

Science

- Gizmos & Gadgets
  The Learning Company
- A.D.A.M. The Inside Story Complete
  adam.com
- Science Court Collection
  Tom Snyder Productions

Social Studies

- Sim City
  Maxis
- TimeLiner
  Tom Snyder Productions
- Where in the *** is Carmen Sandiego
  The Learning Company
- Decisions, Decisions
  Tom Snyder Productions

STANDARDS BY CONTENT AREA

Athletic Coaches

National Standards for Athletic Coaches

National Association for Sport and Physical Education. *National Standards for Athletic Coaches*. (1999). Available online:
http://www.aahperd.org/naspe/publications-coachesstandards.html

Civics and Government

National Standards for Civics and Government

Center for Civic Education. *National Standards for Civics and Government*. (1994). Available online: http://www.civiced.org/

Economic Education

Standards for Economic Education

The National Council on Economic Education (NCEE) in partnership with the National Association of Economic Educators and the Foundation for Teaching Economics. *Voluntary National Content Standards in Economics*. (2000). Available online: http://www.economicsamerica.org/standards/index.html

English/Language Arts

Standards for English Language Arts

National Council of Teachers of English and the International Reading Association. *The Standards for English Language Arts*.
Available online: http://www.ncte.org/standards/standards.shtml
For more information about the standards: http://www.ncte.org/standards/

Foreign Lanaguage

Standards for Foreign Language Learning

American Council on the Teaching of Foreign Languages. *The Standards for Foreign Language Learning*. (1998). Available online:
http://www.accesseric.org/resources/ericreview/vol6no1/standard.html

Geography

National Geography Standards for Grades K–12

National Council for Geographic Education. *The Eighteen National Geography Standards*. (1998). Standards and information about the standards available online:
http://www.ncge.org/publications/tutorial/standards/
http://www.nationalgeographic.com/resources/ngo/education/standards.html

Health

National Health Education Standards/Training

American Association for Health Education. *National Health Education Standards/Training*. (2001). Available online:
http://www.aahperd.org/AAHE/programs-nhestandards.html

Mathematics
Principles and Standards for School Mathematics
National Council of Teachers of Mathematics (NCTM). *Principles and Standards for School Mathematics*. (2000). Available online: http://standards.nctm.org/

Music
National Standards for Music Education
MENC— The National Association for Music Education. *National Standards for Music Education*. Available online: http://www.menc.org/

Physical Education
National Standards for Physical Education
National Association for Sport and Physical Education. *National Standards for Physical Education*. (1999). Available online:
http://www.aahperd.org/NASPE/publications-nationalstandards.html

Science
Science Education Standards
National Academy of Sciences: National Research Council. *National Science Education Standards*. (1995). Available online:
http://books.nap.edu/html/nses/html/index.html

Social Studies
Social Studies Standards
National Council for the Social Studies (NCSS). *Expectations of Excellence: Curriculum Standards for Social Studies*. (1994). Available online:
http://www.ncss.org/standards/toc.html

Technology Standards for K–12 Students
International Society for Technology in Education, NETS*S
International Society for Technology in Education (ISTE). *National Educational Standards for Students*. (2000). Available online:
http://cnets.iste.org/index2.html

Technology Standards for Teachers
International Society for Technology in Education NETS*T
International Society for Technology in Education (ISTE). *National Educational Standards for Teachers*. (2000). Available online:
http://cnets.iste.org/teachstandintro.html

CONTENT AREA STANDARDS
English Language Arts[20]

These standards are presented in a list, However, they are not distinct and separable; they are, in fact, interrelated and should be considered as a whole.

1. Students read a wide range of print and non-print texts to build an understanding of texts, of themselves, and of the cultures of the United States and the world; to acquire new information; to respond to the needs and demands of society and the workplace; and for personal fulfillment. Among these texts are fiction and nonfiction, classic and contemporary works.

2. Students read a wide range of literature from many periods in many genres to build an understanding of the many dimensions (e.g., philosophical, ethical, aesthetic) of human experience.

3. Students apply a wide range of strategies to comprehend, interpret, evaluate, and appreciate texts. They draw on their prior experience, their interactions with other readers and writers, their knowledge of word meaning and of other texts, their word identification strategies, and their understanding of textual features (e.g., sound-letter correspondence, sentence structure, context, graphics).

4. Students adjust their use of spoken, written, and visual language (e.g., conventions, style, vocabulary) to communicate effectively with a variety of audiences and for different purposes.

5. Students employ a wide range of strategies as they write and use different writing process elements appropriately to communicate with different audiences for a variety of purposes.

6. Students apply knowledge of language structure, language conventions (e.g., spelling and punctuation), media techniques, figurative language, and genre to create, critique, and discuss print and nonprint texts.

7. Students conduct research on issues and interests by generating ideas and questions, and by posing problems. They gather, evaluate, and synthesize data from a variety of sources (e.g., print and nonprint texts, artifacts, people) to communicate their discoveries in ways that suit their purpose and audience.

8. Students use a variety of technological and information resources (e.g., libraries, databases, computer networks, video) to gather and synthesize information and to create and communicate knowledge.

9. Students develop an understanding of and respect for diversity in language use, patterns, and dialects across cultures, ethnic groups, geographic regions, and social roles.

10. Students whose first language is not English make use of their first language to develop competency in the English language arts and to develop understanding of content across the curriculum.

11. Students participate as knowledgeable, reflective, creative, and critical members of a variety of literacy communities.

12. Students use spoken, written, and visual language to accomplish their own purposes (e.g., for learning, enjoyment, persuasion, and the exchange of information).

---

[20] **Source:** Reprinted with permission from *Standards for English Language Arts*. Copyright ©1996 by the National Council of Teachers of English. Sponsored by National Council of Teachers of English and the International Reading Association. (http://www.ncte.org

National Geography Standards for Grades K–12[21]

Sponsored by the National Council for Geographic Education, http://www.ncge.org. Information about the standards is available from the National Geographic Society: http://www.nationalgeographic.com/resources/ngo/education/standards.html.

The geographically informed person knows and understands:

The World in Spatial Terms

1. How to use maps and other geographic representations, tools, and technologies to acquire, process, and report information from a spatial perspective.
2. How to use mental maps to organize information about people, places, and environments in a spatial context.
3. How to analyze the spatial organization of people, places, and environments on Earth's surface.

Places and Regions

4. The physical and human characteristics of places.
5. That people create regions to interpret Earth's complexity.
6. How culture and experience influence people's perceptions of places and regions.

Physical Systems

7. The physical processes that shape the patterns of Earth's surface.
8. The characteristics and spatial distribution of ecosystems on Earth's surface.

Human Systems

9. The characteristics, distribution, and migration of human populations on Earth's surface.
10. The characteristics, distribution, and complexity of Earth's cultural mosaics.
11. The patterns and networks of economic interdependency on Earth's surface.
12. The processes, patterns, and functions of human settlement.
13. How the forces of cooperation and conflict among people influence the division and control of Earth's surface.

Environment and Society

14. How human actions modify the physical environment.
15. How physical systems affect human systems.
16. The changes that occur in the meaning, use, distribution, and importance of resources.

The Uses of Geography

17. How to apply geography to interpret the past.
18. How to apply geography to interpret the present and plan for the future.

---

[21] **Source:** Reprinted with permission from *Geography for Life: National Geography Standards.* Copyright ©1994 National Council for Geographic Education. All rights reserved. Available online at http://www.ncge.org/publications/tutorial/standards/

Principles & Standards for School Mathematics[22]

Sponsored by the National Council of Teachers of Mathematics (NCTM). Available online at http://standards.nctm.org/

Number and Operations
Instructional programs from PreK–12 should enable all students to—
- understand numbers, ways of representing numbers, relationships among numbers, and number systems;
- understand meanings of operations and how they relate to one another;
- compute fluently and make reasonable estimate

Algebra
Instructional programs from PreK–12 should enable all students to—
- understand patterns, relations, and functions;
- represent and analyze mathematical situations and structures using algebraic symbols;
- use mathematical models to represent and understand quantitative relationships;
- analyze change in various contexts.

Geometry
Instructional programs from PreK–12 should enable all students to—
- analyze characteristics and properties of two- and three-dimensional geometric shapes and develop mathematical arguments about geometric relationships;
- specify locations and describe spatial relationships using coordinate geometry and other representational systems;
- apply transformations and use symmetry to analyze mathematical situations;
- use visualization, spatial reasoning, and geometric modeling to solve problems.

Measurement
Instructional programs from PreK–12 should enable all students to—
- understand measurable attributes of objects and the units, systems, and processes of measurement;
- apply appropriate techniques, tools, and formulas to determine measurements.

Data Analysis and Probability
Instructional programs from PreK–12 should enable all students to—
- formulate questions that can be addressed with data and collect, organize, and display relevant data to answer them;
- select and use appropriate statistical methods to analyze data;
- develop and evaluate inferences and predictions that are based on data;
- understand and apply basic concepts of probability.

---

[22] Reprinted with permission from *Principles and Standards for School Mathematics*. Copyright ©2000 by the National Council of Teachers of Mathematics. All rights reserved.

Problem Solving
Instructional programs from PreK–12 should enable all students to—
- build new mathematical knowledge through problem solving;
- solve problems that arise in mathematics and in other contexts;
- apply and adapt a variety of appropriate strategies to solve, problems;
- monitor and reflect on the process of mathematical problem solving.

Reasoning and Proof
Instructional programs from PreK–12 should enable all students to—
- recognize reasoning and proof as fundamental aspects of mathematics;
- make and investigate mathematical conjectures;
- develop and evaluate mathematical arguments and proofs;
- select and use various types of reasoning and methods of proof.

Communication
Instructional programs from PreK–12 should enable all students to—
- organize and consolidate their mathematical thinking through communication;
- communicate their mathematical thinking coherently and clearly to peers, teachers, and others;
- analyze and evaluate the mathematical thinking and strategies of others;
- use the language of mathematics to express mathematical ideas precisely.

Connections
Instructional programs from PreK–12 should enable all students to—
- recognize and use connections among mathematical ideas;
- understand how mathematical ideas interconnect and build on one another to produce a coherent whole;
- recognize and apply mathematics in contexts outside of mathematics.

Representation
Instructional programs from PreK–12 should enable all students to—
- create and use representations to organize, record, and communicate mathematical ideas;
- select, apply, and translate among mathematical representations to solve problems;
- use representations to model and interpret physical, social, and mathematical phenomena.

Science Education Standards[23]

Sponsored by the National Academy of Sciences: National Research Council (NAS: NRC). For the complete standards, see NAS:NRC's *National Science Education Standards.* (1995). Available online: http://books.nap.edu/html/nses/html/index.html

Science Content Standards

1. **Unifying Concepts and Processes**

   As a result of activities in grades K–12, all students should develop understanding and abilities aligned with the following concepts and processes:
   - Systems, order, and organization
   - Evidence, models, and explanation
   - Constancy, change, and measurement
   - Evolution and equilibrium
   - Form and function

2. **Science as Inquiry**

   As a result of activities, all students K–12 should develop
   - Abilities necessary to do scientific inquiry
   - Understanding about scientific inquiry

3. **Physical Science**

   As a result of the activities in grades K–4, all students should develop an understanding of
   - Properties of objects and materials
   - Position and motion of objects
   - Light, heat, electricity, and magnetism

   As a result of their activities in grades 5–8, all students should develop an understanding of
   - Properties and changes of properties in matter
   - Motions and forces
   - Transfer of energy

   As a result of their activities in grades 9–12, all students should develop an understanding of
   - Structure of atoms
   - Structure and properties of matter
   - Chemical reactions
   - Motions and forces
   - Conservation of energy and increase in disorder
   - Interactions of energy and matter

---

[23] Reprinted with permission from *National Science Education Standards.* Copyright © 1995, by the National Academy of Sciences. Courtesy of the National Academy Press, Washington, D.C.

4. **Life Science**

As a result of activities in grades K–4, all students should develop understanding of

- The characteristics of organisms
- Life cycles of organisms
- Organisms and environments

As a result of their activities in grades 5–8, all students should develop understanding of

- Structure and function in living systems
- Reproduction and heredity
- Regulation and behavior
- Populations and ecosystems
- Diversity and adaptations of organisms

As a result of their activities in grades 9–12, all students should develop understanding of

- The cell
- Molecular basis of heredity
- Biological evolution
- Interdependence of organisms
- Matter, energy, and organization in living systems
- Behavior of organisms

5. **Earth and Space Science**

As a result of their activities in grades K–4, all students should develop an understanding of

- Properties of earth materials
- Objects in the sky
- Changes in earth and sky

As a result of their activities in grades 5–8, all students should develop an understanding of

- Structure of the earth system
- Earth's history
- Earth in the solar system

As a result of their activities in grades 9–12, all students should develop an understanding of

- Energy in the earth system
- Geochemical cycles
- Origin and evolution of the earth system
- Origin and evolution of the universe

6. **Science and Technology**

As a result of activities in grades K–4, all students should develop

- Abilities of technological design
- Understanding about science and technology

106

• Abilities to distinguish between natural objects and objects made by humans

As a result of activities in grades 5–8, all students should develop
　　• Abilities of technological design
　　• Understandings about science and technology

As a result of activities in grades 9–12, all students should develop
　　• Abilities of technological design
　　• Understandings about science and technology

7. **Science in Personal and Social Perspectives**

As a result of activities in grades K–4, all students should develop understanding of
　　• Personal health
　　• Characteristics and changes in populations
　　• Types of resources
　　• Changes in environments
　　• Science and technology in local challenges

As a result of activities in grades 5–8, all students should develop understanding of
　　• Personal health
　　• Populations, resources, and environments
　　• Natural hazards
　　• Risks and benefits
　　• Science and technology in society

As a result of activities in grades 9–12, all students should develop understanding of
　　• Personal and community health
　　• Population growth
　　• Natural resources
　　• Environmental quality
　　• Natural and human-induced hazards
　　• Science and technology in local, national, and global challenges

8. **History and Nature of Science Standards**

As a result of activities in grades K–12, all students should develop understanding of
　　• Science as a human endeavor

As a result of activities in grades 5–8, all students should develop understanding of
　　• Nature of science
　　• History of science

As a result of activities in grades 9–12, all students should develop understanding of
　　• Nature of scientific knowledge
　　• Historical perspectives

Social Studies Standards[24]

Sponsored by the National Council for the Social Studies (NCSS), the *Expectations of Excellence: Curriculum Standards for Social Studies* (1994) are described and available online: http://www.ncss.org/standards/toc.html

Standards for Grades K–12: Ten Thematic Strands

1. **Culture**: Social studies programs should include experiences that provide for the study of culture and cultural diversity.

2. **Time, Continuity, and Change**: Social studies programs should include experiences that provide for the study of the ways human beings view themselves in and over time.

3. **People, Places, and Environments:** Social studies programs should include experiences that provide for the study of people, places, and environments.

4. **Individual Development and Identity:** Social studies programs should include experiences that provide for the study of individual development and identity.

5. **Individuals, Groups, and Institutions**: Social studies programs should include experiences that provide for the study of interactions among individuals, groups, and institutions.

6. **Power, Authority, and Governance:** Social studies programs should include experiences that provide for the study of how people create and change structures of power, authority, and governance.

7. **Production, Distribution, and Consumption:** Social studies programs should include experiences that provide for the study of how people organize for the production, distribution, and consumption of goods and services.

8. **Science, Technology, and Society:** Social studies programs should include experiences that provide for the study of relationships among science, technology, and society.

9. **Global Connections:** Social studies programs should include experiences that provide for the study of global connections and interdependence.

10. **Civic Ideals and Practice:** Social studies programs should include experiences that provide for the study of the ideals, principles, and practices of citizenship in a democratic republic.

---

[24] Reprinted with permission from *Expectations of Excellence: Curriculum Standards for Social Studies.* Copyright © 1994, by the National Council for the Social Studies. All rights reserved.

GENERAL INFORMATION RESOURCES
Some of Jeri and Tonya's Favorites

The BeeLine: File Formats by Extension: A dictionary of file formats and file extension codes. http://www.bton.com/tb17/formats.html

MyBookmarks.com http://www.mybookmarks.com/
MyBookmarks is an online Bookmark collector

Britannica.com http://www.britannica.com/
An online encyclopedia as well as news and other links.

iTools http://www.apple.com/education/itools/
iTools allows you to develop a Web site to share classroom projects.

KidSafe www.kidsafe.com
Provides safe internet sites for students.

Lycos Photo Center http://www.lycos.com/l/?1f
Lycos provides online photo storage.

QuizStar http://quiz.4teachers.org
QuizStar is an online quiz generator.

RubiStar http://rubistar.4teachers.org/
RubiStar is an online rubric generator.

Webfavorites http://www.webfavorites.com/
Webfavorites provides online file storage and bookmarks.

Teacher Education Favorites

Merrill Education's Links to General Foundations Resources
http://cw.prenhall.com/bookbind/pubbooks/foundations-cluster/
A comprehensive listing of educational foundations links.

Merrill Education's Links to General Methods Resources
http://cw.prenhall.com/bookbind/pubbooks/methods-cluster/
A comprehensive listing of educational methods links.

US Department of Education
http://www.ed.gov/
This site for parents, teaching professionals, students, and others includes sections containing education-related news releases, policy information, learning and teaching resources, and financial resources for students, institutions, schools, districts, and states.

Web Pages for Kids Around the Federal Government
http://www.hhs.gov/families/kids.htm
Several departments of the federal government have kid's pages linked here.

ISTE NATIONAL EDUCATIONAL TECHNOLOGY STANDARDS FOR TEACHERS (NETS*T)[25]

I. **Technology Operations and Concepts:** Teachers demonstrate a sound understanding of technology operations and concepts. Teachers
- demonstrate introductory knowledge, skills, and understanding of concepts related to technology (as described in the ISTE National Educational Technology Standards for Students).
- demonstrate continual growth in technology knowledge and skills to stay abreast of current and emerging technologies.

II. **Planning and Designing Learning Environments and Experiences:** Teachers plan and design effective learning environments and experiences supported by technology. Teachers
- design developmentally appropriate learning opportunities that apply technology-enhanced instructional strategies to support the diverse needs of learners.
- apply current research on teaching and learning with technology when planning learning environments and experiences.
- identify and locate technology resources and evaluate them for accuracy and suitability.
- plan for the management of technology resources within the context of learning activities.
- plan strategies to manage student learning in a technology-enhanced environment.

III. **Teaching, Learning, and the Curriculum:** Teachers implement curriculum plans that include methods and strategies for applying technology to maximize student learning. Teachers
- facilitate technology-enhanced experiences that address content standards and student technology standards.
- use technology to support learner-centered strategies that address the diverse needs of students.
- apply technology to develop students' higher order skills and creativity.
- manage student learning activities in a technology-enhanced environment.

---

[25] Reprinted with permission from *National Educational Technology Standards for Teachers*, Copyright © 2000, ISTE (International Society for Technology in Education), 800.336.5191 (US & Canada) or 541.302.3777 (Int'l), iste@iste.org, www.iste.org. All rights reserved. Permission does not constitute an endorsement by ISTE. For more information about the NETS Project, contact Lajeane Thomas, Director, NETS Project, 318.247.3923, lthomas@latech.edu.

IV. **Assessment and Evaluation:** Teachers apply technology to facilitate a variety of effective assessment and evaluation strategies. Teachers

- apply technology in assessing student learning of subject matter using a variety of assessment techniques.
- use technology resources to collect and analyze data, interpret results, and communicate findings to improve instructional practice and maximize student learning.
- apply multiple methods of evaluation to determine students' appropriate use of technology resources for learning, communication, and productivity.

V. **Productivity and Professional Practice:** Teachers use technology to enhance their productivity and professional practice. Teachers

- use technology resources to engage in ongoing professional development and lifelong learning.
- continually evaluate and reflect on professional practice to make informed decisions regarding the use of technology in support of student learning.
- apply technology to increase productivity.
- use technology to communicate and collaborate with peers, parents, and the larger community in order to nurture student learning.

VI. **Social, Ethical, Legal, and Human Issues:** Teachers understand the social, ethical, legal, and human issues surrounding the use of technology in PK–12 schools and apply that understanding in practice. Teachers

- model and teach legal and ethical practice related to technology use.
- apply technology resources to enable and empower learners with diverse backgrounds, characteristics, and abilities.
- identify and use technology resources that affirm diversity.
- promote safe and healthy use of technology resources.
- facilitate equitable access to technology resources for all students.

ISTE NATIONAL EDUCATIONAL TECHNOLOGY STANDARDS FOR STUDENTS (NETS*S)[26]

1. **Basic Operations and Concepts**
   - Students demonstrate a sound understanding of the nature and operation of technology systems.
   - Students are proficient in the use of technology.

2. **Social, Ethical, and Human Issues**
   - Students understand the ethical, cultural, and societal issues related to technology.
   - Students practice responsible use of technology systems, information, and software.
   - Students develop positive attitudes toward technology uses that support lifelong learning, collaboration, personal pursuits, and productivity.

3. **Technology Productivity Tools**
   - Students use technology tools to enhance learning, increase productivity, and promote creativity.
   - Students use productivity tools to collaborate in constructing technology-enhanced models, prepare publications, and produce other creative works.

4. **Technology Communications Tools**
   - Students use telecommunications to collaborate, publish, and interact with peers, experts, and other audiences.
   - Students use a variety of media and formats to communicate information and ideas effectively to multiple audiences.

5. **Technology Research Tools**
   - Students use technology to locate, evaluate, and collect information from a variety of sources.
   - Students use technology tools to process data and report results.
   - Students evaluate and select new information resources and technological innovations based on the appropriateness for specific tasks.

6. **Technology Problem-solving and Decision-making Tools**
   - Students use technology resources for solving problems and making informed decisions.
   - Students employ technology in the development of strategies for solving problems in the real world.

---

[26] Reprinted with permission from *National Educational Technology Standards for Students— Connecting Curriculum and Technology*, Copyright © 2000, ISTE (International Society for Technology in Education), 800.336.5191 (US & Canada) or 541.302.3777 (Intl), iste@iste.org, www.iste.org. All rights reserved. Permission does not constitute an endorsement by ISTE. For more information about the NETS Project, contact Lajeane Thomas, Director, NETS Project, 318.257.3923, lthomas@latech.edu.